A Little Bird Told Me

Everyday Expressions from Scripture

Timothy Cross

Copyright © T. J. E. Cross, 2015

Paperback ISBN 978-1-78191-553-0
e-pub ISBN: 978-1-78191-574-5
mobi ISBN: 978-1-78191-575-2

Published in 2015
by
Christian Focus Publications Ltd.
Geanies House, Fearn, Ross-shire,
IV20 1TW, Scotland, UK
www.christianfocus.com

Cover design by Daniel van Straaten

Printed by Bell and Bain, Glasgow

MIX
Paper from
responsible sources
FSC® C007785

CONTENTS

Introduction

There is no book to compare with the sixty-six books which comprise the Bible. The Bible is in a category all of its own. Why is the Bible the God of all books? It is so because it is the Book of God. 'All Scripture is God-breathed ...' (2 Tim. 3:16, NIV). The incomparability of the Bible stems from its being no less than the written Word of the living God Himself. The absolute authority of the Bible for all matters concerning belief and practice cannot be separated from the absolute authority of the supreme, sovereign God Himself, who, by His Holy Spirit, caused the Bible to be written.

The Bible is a vast book, yet the message of the Bible is simple. The message of Scripture is the message of salvation. It is centred on God's own Son, the Lord Jesus Christ, and His atoning death on the cross to save sinners. The inspired Word points us to the incarnate Word. If the message of the Bible's 31,173 verses were to be encapsulated in just one verse, the verse would be John 3:16: 'For God so loved the world that He gave His only begotten Son, that whoever believes in Him should not perish but have everlasting life.'

It is a sad fact that the message of the Bible today – especially here in my own land of the United Kingdom – is largely unknown. Christians are in the minority, and biblical illiteracy and ignorance, even among the educated, seems to be at an all-time high. Yet this being said, unbeknown to both speaker and hearer, expressions from the Bible are frequently quoted! Historically, the influence of the Bible has been so great that it has permeated the very fibre of the English language. People quote biblical expressions without knowing that they are doing so.

The following pages focus on some of the expressions from the Bible that have entered into our everyday life and conversation. The sayings' origins are revealed, and something of their meaning and application is explained. The author's prayer is that this will be of interest to both Christians and non-Christians alike. The author's prayer and hope is also that it will cause some to think carefully about the main message of the Bible and ponder the divine purpose behind its writing – 'written that you may believe that Jesus is the Christ, the Son of God, and that believing you may have life in His name' (John 20:31).

History reveals that revivals of Christianity have always gone hand-in-hand with a revival of interest in the Bible. True Christians have an appetite for God's Word. Surely, though, it is also true to say that a revival of interest in the Bible would also spark a revival of Christianity, for the Word of God is living and life-giving, and has power to transform lives and destinies. If the pages that follow catalyse an interest in the Bible, and cause a desire to know the One beyond and behind the sacred pages, the author's labour of love will have been abundantly rewarded.

Timothy Cross
Cardiff, Wales

1

The apple of my eye

The expression 'You are the apple of my eye' has entered into popular poetry and song. The term is used to describe someone who is very dear, precious and special to us. Think, for instance, of a couple on their wedding day, making their marriage vows. There are millions of women in the world, but out of them all, this one woman is uniquely special to this one man. He has chosen just her to be his special, lifelong companion, and has pledged his marital faithfulness to her alone. She is 'the apple of his eye'.

The expression 'The apple of my eye' has a very ancient pedigree. It goes back to the time of Moses some 1,600 years B.C. Amazingly, it refers not to the love and affection which occurs between human beings, but to the love and tender care which Almighty God has burning in His heart for His people. In Deuteronomy 32:9, 10, Moses wrote: 'For the LORD's portion is His people; Jacob is the place of His inheritance. He found him in a desert land and in the wasteland, a howling wilderness; he encircled him, He instructed him, *He kept him as the apple of His eye*' (emphasis mine). Then, many centuries later, after the exile of God's people to Babylon and their subsequent return to Jerusalem to rebuild the temple, in spite of their sin bringing upon them God's righteous chastisement, the covenant love of God for His people was still the same. They were His special people, for we read in Zechariah 2:8 'For thus says the LORD of hosts: "He sent me after glory, to the nations which plunder you; for *he who touches you touches the apple of His eye*."'(emphasis mine).

In Old Testament times, therefore, out of all the peoples and nations of the world, God had His special people – a people whom he had chosen and redeemed for Himself. They were 'the apple of His eye'. This special relationship to Him was not because of any merit in themselves, but solely because of the electing love and sovereign grace of God. God Himself reminded them: 'For you are a holy people to the LORD your God; the LORD your God has chosen you to be a people for Himself, a special treasure above all the peoples on the face of the earth. The LORD did not set His love on you nor choose you because you were more in number than any other people, for you were the least of all peoples; but because the LORD loves you ...' (Deut. 7:6-8).

The love of God for His people is the greatest and most unfathomable mystery of all. That a holy God, all-sufficient in and of Himself, should love sinners and enter into a special relationship with them is beyond belief – but the Bible tells us it is so.

A literal translation of the original Hebrew expression 'the apple of my eye' would read 'the little man of my eye'. It is a reference to the pupil – the delicate and sensitive part of the eye essential for sight and protected by the eyelid. The expression can only be figurative as, while the God of the Bible is all-seeing, He has no physical eyes as, essentially, 'God is Spirit' (John 4:24), that is, without a body. The term, though, while figurative, speaks volumes about the reality of the divine sensitivity of God towards the people whom He loves. The eye is one of the most sensitive parts of the body. A tiny grain of sand in it produces an irritation out of all proportion to the size of the grain. But in the age to come, the Bible reveals, 'God will wipe away every tear from their [that is, His redeemed people's] eyes' (Rev. 7:17).

'He who touches you touches the apple of His eye' (Zech. 2:8). We are dealing here with a term of endearment – with the love

8

of God for His children. The Christian's salvation is due solely to the love of God. The initiative in salvation is always with God and not with us. His love for us always precedes our love for Him. Our love for Him is always a response to His love for us. 'In this is love, not that we loved God, but that He loved us and sent His Son to be the propitiation for our sins ... We love Him because He first loved us. (1 John 4:10, 19). The Bible reveals that salvation is actually a result of the triune love of the triune God. If we rejoice in God's salvation, it is because, in love, God the Father chose us to be saved before the foundation of the world and in His love sent His Son to die to procure our salvation – 'Christ also has loved us and given Himself for us' (Eph. 5:2). Then, in God's providential timing, He sent His Holy Spirit upon us to apply the work of Christ's salvation to our hearts, bestowing on us saving faith in the crucified Saviour. 'The love of God has been poured out in our hearts by the Holy Spirit who was given to us' (Rom. 5:5).

Christians, therefore, are most certainly 'the apple of God's eye', because they are the recipients and beneficiaries of the triune love of the triune God – 'elect according to the foreknowledge of God the Father, in sanctification of the Spirit, for obedience and sprinkling of the blood of Jesus Christ' (1 Pet. 1:2).

Amidst the turmoil of his life, David prayed to God, 'Keep me as the apple of Your eye; hide me under the shadow of Your wings' (Ps. 17:8). This is a good prayer for us to make when we are aware of our weakness and vulnerability in this difficult and dangerous world. If we belong to Jesus, we may be assured and reassured that we are not mere pawns at the mercy of 'the slings and arrows of outrageous fortune'.[1] We are loved by God. We are

---

1. Shakespeare, Hamlet 3:1

safe under His providential care. He regards us as 'the apple of His eye' (Zech. 2:8). He Himself says 'Yes, I have loved you with an everlasting love …' (Jer. 31:3). On the authority of the Bible one may say: 'He cares for you' (1 Pet. 5:7).

> *Loved with everlasting love,*
> *Led by grace that love to know;*
> *Spirit breathing from above*
> *Thou hast taught me it is so.*
> *O this full and perfect peace!*
> *O this transport all divine!*
> *In a love that cannot cease,*
> *I am His and He is mine!*

(GEORGE WADE ROBINSON, 1838–77)

2

No room at the Inn

It was lunchtime when I was in college. A friend suggested that we go into town for a quick burger. Arriving at the fast-food outlet, the queue extended from the counter to the door. Had we joined it, we would have been late for our afternoon lecture. 'No room at the inn' – said my friend. 'We'll try somewhere else.'

Most would know that the expression 'No room at the inn' is connected with the Christmas story – with the Nativity of Christ – for Christmas is still widely celebrated in the West, even if it is celebrated in a non-Christian way, to use an oxymoron. The expression originates from Luke's account of the birth of Christ. Luke 2:7 reads 'And [Mary] brought forth her firstborn Son, and wrapped Him in swaddling cloths, and laid Him in a manger, because *there was no room for them in the inn*' (emphasis mine).

Luke 2:7 is the only verse in the Bible indicating that the Lord Jesus was born in an animal shelter which contained feeding troughs. Early tradition says He was born in a cave – a cave used for sheltering animals. The Church of the Nativity in Bethlehem, built on the supposed site of Christ's birth, contains a cave or grotto which marks the site of this momentous event.

Why was the Lord of glory born in an animal shelter? The Scripture clues are sparse. Bethlehem was crowded with visitors, for Caesar's decree had ordered people to return to their place of ancestral origin for official government registration. Accommodation in Bethlehem was thus at a premium. The guest rooms at the town's inn were either full, or perhaps the innkeeper – who is not actually mentioned in Scripture – had qualms about giving hospitality to a woman about to give birth. Either way, Mary and Joseph had no choice but to spend the night lodging in the covered shelter provided for animals. Amazingly, it was there – amidst mute beasts and perhaps animal work-hands – that the very Son of God and longed-for Messiah was born. For Mary, this was no doubt both physically distressing and socially humiliating. It was no modern maternity ward, yet the Bible tells us that it was in that animal shelter that Christ was born. There, Mary 'brought forth her firstborn Son, and wrapped Him in swaddling cloths, and laid Him in a manger, because *there was no room for them in the inn'* (emphasis mine).

The Reality of Christ's Birth

Who would ever have thought that the Son of God would have been born in the way that He was? Christ's birth in an animal shelter just could not have been invented by human imagination. 'Lo! Within a manger lies, He who built the starry skies.'[1] It shows that the Christian faith is based on history, not mythology. Here we are dealing with reality, not fantasy. Our calendars prove the reality of Christ's birth every day, for we are living in the twenty-first century A.D. – after the birth of Christ. As Peter wrote some years later, 'We did not follow cunningly devised fables when we made known to you the power and coming of our Lord Jesus Christ' (2 Pet. 1:16).

The Humility of Christ's Birth

In 2 Corinthians 8:9 we read, 'For you know the grace of our Lord Jesus Christ, that though He was rich, yet for your sakes He became poor, that you through His poverty might become rich.' Theologians divide Christ's life into two states: His state

---

1. Edward Caswall, (1814–78)

of humiliation and His state of exaltation. His birth in the 'cattle shed' fits into the former category.

> 'Christ's humiliation consisted in His being born, and that in a low condition, made under the law, undergoing the miseries of this life, the wrath of God and the cursed death of the cross; in being buried, and continuing under the power of death for a time.'[2]

That there was 'no room in the inn' for Christ tallies with Isaiah's ancient prophecy that 'He is despised and rejected by men' (Isa. 53:3). Christ was rejected at His birth, and then throughout His life. His rejection culminated in His being nailed to a plank of wood and hung up to die, and then for three hours He was even forsaken by God the Father Himself. His rejection, however, wrought our reconciliation. His forsakenness wrought our forgiveness. It was not accidental but providential. It was all part of God's eternal plan to save a people for Himself and for His glory.

The Glory of Christ's Birth

In Jesus, God became man – 'the Word became flesh and dwelt among us' (John 1:14). The Son of God became a son of man that the sons of men might become the sons of God. He was born that we might be born again. He was born to die, so that dying sinners might have eternal life. The incarnation of Christ is a vital link in the chain of salvation history. The gospel proclaims, 'For God so loved the world that He gave His only begotten Son, that whoever believes in Him should not perish but have everlasting life' (John 3:16).

The glory of Christ's birth stems from the fact that He was born to be our Saviour. 'There is born to you this day in the city of David a Savior, who is Christ the Lord' (Luke 2:11) –

---

2. *The Westminster Shorter Catechism,* Question 27

a Saviour from sin, a Saviour from the wrath of God, a Saviour from eternal hell.

No room at the inn! The glory of Christ's birth is not immediately evident to the eye, but well known to the eye of faith. He was born in unusual circumstances and surroundings – an animal shelter. 'laid … in a manger because there was no room for them in the inn.' It begs the evangelistic question; 'Have you any room for Jesus?'

> *Thou didst leave Thy throne*
> *And Thy kingly crown,*
> *When Thou camest to earth for me;*
> *But in Bethlehem's home*
> *Was found no room*
> *For Thy holy nativity!*
>
> *O come to my heart, Lord Jesus,*
> *There is room in my heart for Thee.*

(EMILY ELLIOTT, 1836–97)

3

The writing is on the wall

The expression 'The writing's on the wall' is commonly used to refer to some envisaged trouble ahead, judging from a present action or situation. For example, 'The writing's on the wall for you if you do not give up smoking.' The expression has even been heard in relation to a football team on a losing streak – 'Relegation surely awaits them. Their current form suggests the writing's on the wall.'

The Divine Graffiti of Daniel

The expression 'the writing is on the wall' originates from the Book of Daniel in the Old Testament. Daniel relates some divine graffiti, no less – a time when God Himself actually wrote on a wall. The background to all this is as follows:

The people of Israel had been conquered by the Babylonians under King Nebuchadnezzar. Many of them – including the godly prophet Daniel – were taken from the promised land into exile in Babylon. The Babylonian exile was a sad time in Israel's history – a time of disruption and sorrow. The holy temple at Jerusalem had been destroyed and the children of Israel found themselves in an alien land, surrounded by idols. Psalm 137:1 gives us an insight into the mood of that time when it relates 'By the rivers of Babylon, there we sat down, yea, we wept when we remembered Zion.'

While in Babylon, the Scriptures record, 'Belshazzar the king made a great feast for a thousand of his lords, and drank wine in the presence of the thousand' (Dan. 5:1). This feast was no polite dinner party, but more like a drunken orgy. As the feast went on,

Belshazzar got less and less inhibited, and 'While he tasted the wine, Belshazzar gave the command to bring the gold and silver vessels which his father Nebuchadnezzar had taken from the temple which had been in Jerusalem, that the king and his lords, his wives, and his concubines might drink from them. Then they brought the gold vessels that had been taken from the temple of the house of God which had been in Jerusalem; and the king and his lords, his wives, and his concubines drank from them. They drank wine, and praised the gods of gold and silver, bronze and iron, wood and stone' (Dan. 5:2 ff.).

King Belshazzar thus used the holy vessels of the Jerusalem temple for unholy and idolatrous purposes. In doing so, he revealed his disrespect and even contempt for the God of Israel. Did this matter, though? Was not Belshazzar the king of Babylon, and thus 'free to do his own thing'? No. The Bible then relates the instance of divine graffiti which is the subject of this chapter: 'In the same hour the fingers of a man's hand appeared and wrote opposite the lampstand on the plaster of the wall of the king's palace ...' (Dan. 5:5). King Belshazzar sobered up in an instant. He knew that this was the hand of God in judgment. 'Then the king's countenance changed, and his thoughts troubled him, so that the joints of his hips were loosened and his knees knocked against each other' (Dan. 5:6). 'King Belshazzar was greatly troubled, his countenance was changed, and his lords were astonished' (Dan. 5:9).

When the king's wise men and counsellors failed to interpret the writing on the wall, godly Daniel was brought in before him to explain the words from the divine fingers. Daniel was an intimate friend of the true God, and boldly rebuked and reprimanded Belshazzar for his sacrilege. Daniel was blunt, and told the king, 'the God who holds your breath in His hand and owns all your ways, you have not glorified' (Dan. 5:23). The words from heaven were 'MENE, MENE, TEKEL, UPHARSIN' (Dan. 5:25). Daniel explained to the king, 'This is the interpretation of each word. MENE: God has numbered your kingdom, and finished it; TEKEL: You have been weighed in the balances, and found wanting; PERES: Your kingdom has been divided, and given to the Medes and Persians' (Dan. 5:26 ff.). Belshazzar, then, was under the judgment of God. His number was up. He had been weighed in the balances and found wanting. The prophetical 'writing on the wall' was fulfilled without delay. God took away Belshazzar's life and kingship, for, 'That very night Belshazzar, king of the Chaldeans, was slain. And Darius the Mede received the kingdom, being about sixty-two years old' (Dan. 5:30, 31).

'The writing is on the wall …' Truth be told, the bad news is that 'the writing is on the wall' for us as much as it was for King Belshazzar of Babylon. This is so because we will all die one day and face God in judgment. 'It is appointed for men to die once, but after this the judgment' (Heb. 9:27). Belshazzar showed contempt for God. But all sin shows contempt for God. All sin dishonours God because sin is a flouting of His commandments and a rebellion against His divine authority. And we are all sinners, for the Bible says, 'There is none righteous, no, not one' (Rom. 3:10); 'for all have sinned and fall short of the glory of God' (Rom. 3:23).

Sadly, therefore, 'the writing is on the wall' for each one of us, because we are all sinners in the hands of an angry God who cannot tolerate sin, but only judge it. Is there any hope for us at all then? The Bible says that there is, because there is a gospel of divine grace. The Christian gospel proclaims that we may escape from the judgment of God through the mercy of God. He actually sent His own Son into the world to die in the place of sinners and turn aside His wrath from against them. The death of Christ at Calvary is the ultimate expression of both the love and the wrath of God, for, because of Calvary, God is able both to condemn sin and spare the sinner who believes in Jesus. 'But God demonstrates His own love toward us, in that while we were still sinners, Christ died for us' (Rom. 5:8).

Yes, we deserve to be punished for our sins – but there is a Saviour! 'Jesus who delivers us from the wrath to come' (1 Thess. 1:10). The Bible affirms that if our faith is in Jesus and His atoning death for our sins, sinners though we are, all is eternally well with us. Jesus was judged for our justification. He was condemned for our eternal consolation. 'There is therefore now no condemnation to those who are in Christ Jesus' (Rom. 8:1).

'The writing's on the wall ...' It was for King Belshazzar in ancient Babylon, and it is for every one of us today. Hence the urgency of the evangelistic task. Hence the absolute necessity of saving faith in Jesus.

4

The powers that be

'Daft. Due to Health and Safety Regulations, the powers that be have forbidden children to hold conker matches in the school playground.' 'The powers that be have put a speed camera on the road near me.' 'I was looking forward to retiring, but the powers that be have gone and raised the retirement age.'

We use the term 'the powers that be' to refer to some rules, regulations or laws that have come our way, which we have no choice but to obey if we do not want to land ourselves in trouble. If we do not like, or do not see the point or purpose of the rule, such obedience can 'grate on us'. But we give our reluctant assent to the anonymous legislators who have stipulated what is to be so. We thus go along with 'the powers that be'.

The expression 'the powers that be' originates in the thirteenth chapter of the Book of Romans in the New Testament. Here, the Apostle Paul, under the inspiration of the Holy Spirit, gives us what is to be the Christian attitude to the government of the day under which we find ourselves. In Romans 13:1, Paul states 'the powers that be [that is, human government] are ordained of God' (KJV). This being so, Paul enjoins submission and obedience to the government of the day because, seeing as government is 'of God', rebellion against the civil government is actually rebellion against God. Christians, therefore, are to be characterized by civic and civil responsibility. They are to be upright, law-abiding citizens of the country in which God has placed them, helping, rather than hindering its smooth running. Paul's full statement and explanation of our attitude towards 'the powers that be' is as follows:

'Let every soul be subject unto the higher powers. For there is no power but of God: the powers that be are ordained of God. Whosoever therefore resisteth the power, resisteth the ordinance of God: and they that resist shall receive to themselves damnation. For rulers are not a terror to good works, but to the evil. Wilt thou then not be afraid of the power? do that which is good, and thou shalt have praise of the same. For he is the minister of God to thee for good. But if thou do that which is evil, be afraid; for he beareth not the sword in vain: for he is the minister of God, a revenger to execute wrath upon him that doeth evil. Wherefore ye must needs be subject, not only for wrath, but also for conscience sake. For for this cause pay ye tribute also: for they are God's ministers, attending continually upon this very thing. Render therefore to all their dues: tribute to whom tribute is due; custom to whom custom; fear to whom fear; honour to whom honour' (Rom. 13:1-7, KJV).

Lawful Authority

The Bible teaches that it is the will of God that we all obey the lawful authority ordained by God, whether this authority is invested in our parents, teachers, pastors, employer, the police or the government of the day. All are ordained for our benefit. The God of the Bible is the ultimate Authority – but He exercises this authority by delegating it to human beings. The God of the Bible is a God of law and order and states 'Let all things be done decently and in order' (1 Cor. 14:40). The opposite of law and order is lawlessness and disorder. When the harmonious way of heaven is cast aside, the misery and anarchy of hell is sure to ensue. Christians are thus to be subject to the government of the day, even when they do not personally like the 'colours' of the government of the day.

When Paul wrote Romans 13, the Emperor Nero was in power. Nero had a pathological hatred of Christians and eventually took Paul's life. But Paul still enjoined submission. He never encouraged so-called 'civil disobedience'. God had put Nero in power. He and his officers were there to restrain evil and promote good. Rather than opening our mouths to complain about the government, or getting on our feet to protest against the government, the Bible would rather have us get on our knees to pray for the government: Pray that its members would seek wisdom from God and legislate in a way pleasing to Him. Pray that conditions conducive to the spread of the gospel would be promoted. We remember (in the famous words of Alfred, Lord Tennyson) that 'More things are wrought by prayer than this world dreams of.' Hence Paul wrote to Timothy, 'Therefore I exhort first of all that supplications, prayers, intercessions, and giving of thanks be made for all men, for kings and all who are in authority, that we may lead a quiet and peaceable life in all godliness and reverence' (1 Tim. 2:1, 2).

Is it ever right to rebel?
Christians, then, are subject to 'the powers that be'. Unquestioningly and uncritically so? Not quite. There is one exception to this. If the government orders us to disobey the revealed will of God in the Bible, it has overstepped its mark. If the government of the day orders us to do something contrary to God's Word, we may disobey out of obedience to the Higher Authority – out of obedience to God Himself. An example of this occurred during the life of the early church. Christ had commanded His people to preach the gospel. The religious authorities 'called

them and commanded them not to speak at all nor teach in the name of Jesus. But Peter and John answered and said to them, "Whether it is right in the sight of God to listen to you more than to God, you judge"' (Acts 4:18, 19). Needless to say, the apostles carried on preaching the gospel. They rebelled against the human authority when it clashed with the divine. Such is incumbent on all Christians if needs be. 'We ought to obey God rather than men' (Acts 5:29).

Martyrdom

The early Christians generally submitted to 'the powers that be' – the Roman government of their day. When they were required to offer incense to Caesar, though, and say, 'Caesar is Lord,' conscience forbade their doing so. Their conviction was that 'Jesus is Lord.' Worshipping Caesar would have meant committing the sin of idolatry. They thus rebelled, and their rebellion cost them their lives. They were martyred for the Christian faith – literally, thrown to the lions…

May God give us grace to follow Christ whatever the consequence or cost. We, under God, are subject to 'the powers that be'. But our ultimate allegiance is to King Jesus the 'KING OF KINGS AND LORD OF LORDS' (Rev. 19:16) to whom, one day, every knee shall bow.

5

God forbid!

'God forbid!' Considering that we live in a predominantly secular age in which – to quote a former Prime Minister's spokesman – 'We don't do God', it is perhaps surprising how often this expression is heard. The words are used to express an abhorrence at the possibility that a certain thing might happen. 'If the current economic conditions continue – God forbid – we will have to make redundancies.' 'I've taken out medical insurance lest – God forbid – I fall ill when I'm on holiday.' 'Two ambulances are on standby at the show, lest – God forbid – any of the boxers get seriously injured.' 'God' is thus invoked even by those who do not really believe in Him. Lip service is paid to the possibility that He – not ourselves – is the one who controls the events of time and space.

The expression 'God forbid' is used often in the Bible. Significantly, in Galatians 6:14 the Apostle Paul lays bare the outlook of his life and heart when he asserts 'But *God forbid* that I should boast except in the cross of our Lord Jesus Christ, by whom the world has been crucified to me, and I to the world' (emphasis mine).

The words translated 'God forbid' here are a translation of the Greek optative mood. They express a strong wish. Everyone glories in something or someone. Paul here is expressing the strong desire that he would never glory in anything but the crucified Christ – that the cross of Christ and the Christ of the cross alone would be his life's obsession and absorption. In fact, this all-embracing interest of Paul's expressed here in Galatians 6:14 made the world around him as good as dead to him. And his fixation with the Christ of Calvary also made him as good as 'dead' to others – strangers to Christ's salvation just could not understand Paul's world view and outlook when he gloried in a crucified Messiah and considered 'everything as loss because of the surpassing worth of knowing Christ Jesus my Lord' (Phil. 3:8, ESV). For Paul, the very best this world had to offer was 'rubbish' when put alongside Christ and His salvation.

Glorying in the Cross

'God forbid that I should boast except in the cross of our Lord Jesus Christ ...' (Gal. 6:14). Paul's desire here was considered strange by many. Crucifixion was the most shameful form of capital punishment. Paul relates 'the offence [literally, the scandal] of the cross' (Gal. 5:11). Yet Paul's desire is shared by every true Christian, for every true Christian glories in the cross of Christ and the Christ of the cross. Why? Because the cross of Christ alone is the ground of our eternal salvation – the ground of our eternal acceptance with God. The technical term for this is 'justification'. A Christian is one who is 'justified by His blood' (Rom. 5:9). *The Westminster Shorter Catechism* describes justification in these words: 'Justification is an act of God's free grace wherein He pardoneth all our sins and accepteth us as righteous in His sight, only for the righteousness of Christ imputed to us, and received by faith alone.'[1]

Galatians

Paul's letter to the Galatians – from which our expression comes – is perhaps the earliest of his letters in the New Testament. Its theme is the same as that of Romans: justification by the grace of God. Whereas Romans is a calm and reasoned explanation of justification, Paul's language in Galatians is much more forceful and urgent. In Romans, he explains justification doctrinally, but in Galatians Paul is forced to defend justification controversially. In Galatians, Paul uses strong language, as the doctrine of justification by God's grace was under threat. There were false teachers in the province of Galatia who taught that justification – our

---

1. *The Westminster Shorter Catechism,* Question 33

acceptance with God – is based on what we do. They preached a 'salvation' by human works. The matter never goes away. How many today believe that heaven is gained by 'doing the best you can' – or even 'justification by respectability'.

Paul's strong objection to 'justification by works' was because it bypasses the cross of Christ which is at the heart of the Christian faith. He thus wrote, 'I do not set aside the grace of God; for if righteousness comes through the law, then Christ died in vain' (Gal. 2:21). He is saying that if we could gain salvation by what we do, then the work of Christ on the cross was not necessary. The Christian gospel, however, proclaims that it is Christ's finished work on the cross that saves – not our imperfect, unfinished works. Salvation is not a matter of 'do' but 'done' – for 'Done is the work that saves.'

The Cross in Galatians
The cross of Christ and its saving benefits permeate Paul's epistle to the Galatians. It was Paul's way of countering those who believed and taught that salvation could be gained by some other way:

> *'our Lord Jesus Christ … gave Himself for our sins, that He might deliver us from this present evil age'* (Gal. 1:3, 4).

> *'a man is not justified by the works of the law but by faith in Jesus Christ'* (Gal. 2:16).

> *'the Son of God … loved me and gave Himself for me'* (Gal. 2:20).

> *'Christ has redeemed us from the curse of the law, having become a curse for us (for it is written, "Cursed is everyone who hangs on a tree")'* (Gal. 3:13).

'God sent forth His Son ... to redeem those who were under the law, that we might receive the adoption as sons' (Gal. 4:4, 5).

'Christ has made us free' (Gal. 5:1).

Paul knew the damnable folly of salvation by works. And Paul knew the glorious reality of salvation by the finished work of Christ on the cross. He had experienced it; he gloried in it and he proclaimed it. His life's work entailed exhorting others to trust the crucified Saviour, and know the forgiveness of sins and peace with God which only the cross of Christ can bestow.

Christianity is 'crosstianity'. At the heart of the Christian faith lies the cross of Christ – His death in the place of sinners; His death to save sinners from eternal death. Knowing the salvation which flows from Christ's cross, therefore, every Christian is one with Paul in saying, 'But *God forbid* that I should boast except in the cross of our Lord Jesus Christ ...' (Gal. 6:14, emphasis mine).

Isaac Watts was one of many people saved by the grace of God in Christ on the cross. He became an effective preacher of the same wonderful grace which had saved him. He also wrote a famous hymn, often sung at communion services – one to which all Christians can relate. It includes the lines:

> *Forbid it, Lord, that I should boast,*
> *Save in the death of Christ my God!*
> *All the vain things that charm me most,*
> *I sacrifice them to His blood.*
>
> *Were the whole realm of nature mine,*
> *That were a present far too small!*
> *Love so amazing, so divine,*
> *Demands my soul, my life, my all!*

(ISAAC WATTS, 1674–1748)

6

God willing

The expression 'God willing' is an expression confined to Christian circles – although Muslims too say 'Insha'Allah' or 'inshallah' – 'If it please God/Allah.'

A very godly Christian I once knew, when I lived in Northern Ireland, used to pepper her conversation with the expression 'D.V.' These initials stand for the Latin *Deo Volente* – which means 'God willing', or, more loosely, 'If the Lord wills.'

If we know our Bibles, we will know that 'D.V.' originates from a verse in the New Testament, James 4:15, which states, 'If the Lord wills, we shall live and do this or that.'

'If the Lord wills...' The phrase reminds us that we are not in charge of our own destinies, but completely dependent upon God for all things. He is 'the God who holds your breath in His hand and owns all your ways' (Dan. 5:23). The last words of Timothy McVeigh, the Oklahoma bomber, before he went to the electric chair were: 'I am the master of my fate and the captain of my soul.' How wrong he was!

Who knows what awaits us in the days, weeks and months ahead? Only God does. We may have our hopes and plans, but they are subject to God's overall plan, whether we like it or not. 'A man's heart plans his way, but the LORD directs his steps' (Prov. 16:9). 'A man's steps are of the LORD; how then can a man understand his own way?' (Prov. 20:24).

A joke in Jewish circles goes something like this: Question: 'How do you make the Almighty laugh?' Answer: 'Tell Him your plans.' A Christian will certainly agree with the spirit of that joke, for we may propose, but God is perfectly entitled to dispose, for

He is the God who is over all, 'who works all things according to the counsel of His will' (Eph. 1:11). Truth be told, if we could only remember that even our disappointments are His appointments, they would be a lot easier to bear.

'D.V.' Saying this is a recognition that all our lives are under God's control and subject to His will:

> *God holds the key of all unknown*
> *And I am glad.*
> *If other hands should hold the key,*
> *Or if He trusted it to me,*
> *I might be sad.*
>
> *I cannot read His future plans*
> *But this I know:*
> *I have the smiling of His face,*
> *And all the refuge of His grace,*
> *While here below.*

(JOSEPH PARKER, 1830–1902)

Every text has a context

'If the Lord wills ...' It is a good motto to have and be gripped by. Let us read the verses before and after the phrase, so putting the verse into its context. James 4:13-16 states:

'Come now, you who say, "Today or tomorrow we will go to such and such a city, spend a year there, buy and sell, and make a profit"; whereas you do not know what will happen tomorrow. For what is your life? It is even a vapour that appears for a little time and then vanishes away. Instead you ought to say, "If the Lord wills, we shall live and do this or that." But now you boast in your arrogance. All such boasting is evil.'

The context of the verse is the uncertainly and fragility of life. A man has great plans to go into a certain town and spend a year there and get rich in the process. He believes that his business idea is a sure-fire winner. Such plans seem very sound, his friends assure him … But such plans do not account for the fact that Almighty God may take our ability to earn our own living away from us. It is his prerogative even to take away our very life. From a divine perspective, there is no such thing as a premature death. Our gifts, talents, health, wealth and life could be taken away right now if God saw fit. He may see fit to cut us down to size, and give us a right sense of our own importance and His supreme importance. He alone is God!

Notice, though, that the context of our text includes the brevity of life as well as its fragility. 'For what is your life? It is even a vapour that appears for a little time and then vanishes away.' Life itself is brief and fragile. British people will never forget the death of Princess Diana. She was only in her thirties. Who would have thought that on that evening in Paris, when Princess Diana put on her expensive clothes and jewellery, and went out for an expensive meal with Dodi Al Fayed, that these would be her last moments on earth? All of our lives, though, from the princess to the pauper, are subject to the will of God. Saying 'D.V.' – 'if the Lord wills' – acknowledges this fact. David confessed 'I trust in You, O LORD; I say, "You are my God." My times are in Your hand' (Ps. 31:14, 15). The exact number of the days which we shall live on this earth has already been predetermined by Almighty God. 'In Your book they all were written, the days fashioned for me, when as yet there was none of them' (Ps. 139:16).

Trust in the Lord

God willing. Our future hopes and plans are certainly subject to the will of God – 'For of Him and through Him and to Him are all things' (Rom. 11:36).

If we belong to the Lord Jesus, though, we need not fear. Safely under our heavenly Father's loving sway, we are encouraged to trust His providence, and submit to whatever He sends our way, knowing that He is too wise to make mistakes, and too good to be unkind. Scripture affirms: 'We know that all things work together for good to those who love God, to those who are the called according to His purpose' (Rom. 8:28) – and who are we to make ourselves the sole exception to this?

God willing. It is a good motto to remember and an anchor for our souls, for all of our plans are subject to the sovereign will of God.

> *All the way my Saviour leads me,*
> *What have I to ask beside?*
> *Can I doubt His tender mercy*
> *Who through life has been my guide?*
> *Heavenly peace, divinest comfort,*
> *Here by faith in Him to dwell.*
> *For I know whate'er befall me,*
> *Jesus doeth all things well!*

(FRANCES JANE VAN ALSTYNE [FANNY CROSBY], 1820–1915)

7

'He's been made a scapegoat ...'

In popular usage, a 'scapegoat' refers to someone who takes the blame for the failings and faults of others. It seems as if we always have to have someone else to blame! When a football team loses, for instance, the manager may appear on the TV and blame the referee for what he considers a poor decision which lost his team the match. He thus makes the referee a 'scapegoat' for his side's loss. When a country goes through a hard time – the economy takes a dip, unemployment is high, the trains don't run on time, crime is on the rise, etc. ... the blame is put by many firmly on the shoulders of the Prime Minister of the day. The Prime Minister and Government are thus made 'scapegoats'. Also, in the claustrophobic confines of a stressful office, you might hear a murmur of complaint from someone: 'It's not my fault. I'm just being made a scapegoat.'

The idea of the 'scapegoat' originates back in the time of Moses. The scapegoat was actually not man's idea but God's. It was His gracious provision and ordinance. It was His merciful provision for sinners – so that sinners could have fellowship with Him. A holy God can have nothing to do with sin except righteously judge it, so, unless sin is put away, fellowship with Him is impossible. The purpose of the scapegoat was so that human sin could be dealt with and peace with God be made.

The Day of Atonement
It is in Leviticus 16 that we find the details concerning the scapegoat. Once a year, on the 'Day of Atonement', God's instructions

involved taking two goats. One of the goats was to be sacrificed – slain as an offering for sin. But the other goat was kept alive. 'Aaron shall lay both his hands on the head of the live goat, confess over it all the iniquities of the children of Israel, and all their transgressions, concerning all their sins, putting them on the head of the goat, and shall send it away into the wilderness by the hand of a suitable man. The goat shall bear on itself all their iniquities to an uninhabited land; and he shall release the goat in the wilderness' (Lev. 16:21, 22).

Type and Antitype

With our complete Bible, we know that the true 'Scapegoat' is the Lord Jesus Christ. The scapegoat of the Old Testament economy was a picture and prefiguration of the Christ who was to come. The scapegoat of Old Testament times took away sin, but not permanently. The ritual had to be repeated every year. But when Christ came, His sacrifice of Himself at Calvary dealt with our sin once and for all, putting it away from God's sight permanently and also ending the need for any atoning sacrifice to be offered ever again. Christ brought all the types, shadows and promises of the Old Testament to their fulfilment and completion – 'For all the promises of God in Him are Yes, and in Him Amen …' (2 Cor. 1:20).

A scapegoat – as we have intimated – is one who bears the blame and liability of others. This is what Christ did at Calvary. His death was substitutionary. He bore the punishment for the sins of the believer to save the believer from that punishment. He was made accountable for our sin.

'But now, once at the end of the ages, He has appeared to put away sin by the sacrifice of Himself' (Heb. 9:26).

'He's been made a scapegoat ...'

'Christ was offered once to bear the sins of many' (Heb. 9:28).

'...who Himself bore our sins in His own body on the tree' (1 Pet. 2:24).

So thank God for *the* Scapegoat. If our faith is in Jesus, we are exonerated from all blame, for the fearful wrath of God which is our due fell on Him.

On the Day of Atonement, the scapegoat bore the people's sin away into the wilderness, out of their sight. It is Jesus who removes the sin – which condemns us – out of God's sight. He is 'The Lamb of God who takes away the sin of the world' (John 1:29). 'You know that He was manifested to take away our sins, and in Him there is no sin' (1 John 3:5). Because of Jesus, our sins are removed 'As far as the east is from the west, so far has He removed our transgressions from us' (Ps. 103:12). In dying for our sins in our place, Christ was made the ultimate Scapegoat. It is the central doctrine of the Bible and the theme of a thousand hymns.

> *O Christ, what burdens bowed Thy head,*
> *Our load was laid on Thee.*
> *Thou stoodest in the sinner's stead,*
> *Didst bear all ill for me.*
> *A Victim led, Thy blood was shed,*
> *Now there's no load for me!*
>
> *Jehovah lifted up His rod,*
> *O Christ, it fell on Thee.*
> *Thou wast sore stricken of Thy God,*
> *There's not one stroke for me!*
> *Thy tears, Thy blood beneath it flowed,*
> *Thy bruising healeth me!*

A Little Bird Told Me

Jehovah bade His sword awake,
O Christ, it woke 'gainst Thee.
Thy blood the flaming blade must slake,
Thy heart its sheath must be!
All for my sake my peace to make,
Now sleeps that sword for me!

(ANNE ROSS COUSIN, 1824–1906)

8

Worthy of his hire

The biblical expression 'the labourer is worthy of his hire' (Luke 10:7, KJV) is sometimes used in conjunction with the non-biblical expression 'A fair day's work for a fair day's pay'. It is exceedingly rare to meet a person who believes he is overpaid for the work he does! Most of us, though, would like to think that, if we are in paid employment, we are worthy of employing. In the U.K. there is a minimum wage laid down by law. This is designed to protect workers from exploitation. As of writing, the minimum wage stands at £6.19 per hour.

Words from the Master

The expression 'the labourer is worthy of his hire' (Luke 10:7) was originally spoken by the Lord Jesus. The context was that of His saving mission in the world. He had just appointed seventy of His followers to go out into the spiritual harvest field and proclaim the gospel. How, though, were the seventy to be physically sustained when they were out on their work? Even the most spiritual work requires that the worker be clothed and fed. The workers were to trust God to supply their needs, and also to accept the 'means' God provided through human channels. They were to accept the hospitality and provision given to them as they went about their labours without embarrassment, 'For the labourer is worthy of his hire.'

Words from the Apostle

At a later date, the Apostle Paul took up the words of the Lord Jesus and, under the guidance of the Holy Spirit, applied them to the gospel age when local churches are established and nurtured.

Paul stated: 'Even so the Lord has commanded that those who preach the gospel should live from the gospel' (1 Cor. 9:14). Paradoxically, the gospel provides the Lord's servants with the means to eat, so that by eating they can continue to proclaim the gospel. Then in 1 Timothy 5:17, 18 Paul, in a local church context, writes: 'Let the elders who rule well be counted worthy of double honour, especially those who labour in the word and doctrine. For the Scripture says … "The labourer is worthy of his wages".'

If a physician deserves to be paid for his work in caring for people's physical health, does not a pastor deserve to be paid for caring for souls? A surgeon uses his God-given gifts to save lives. By using his God-given gifts, a pastor or an evangelist is instrumental in saving souls. Both thus need and deserve physical and financial support in what they do so they can continue to do what they do.

Workers not shirkers

'The labourer is worthy of his hire.' We can apply these words of the Lord Jesus to a wider context. Work is a divine ordinance as well as a human convenience. There was work to be done even in Eden before the Fall, for 'The LORD God took the man and put him in the garden of Eden to tend and keep it' (Gen. 2:15). The world of employment is one of the major theatres in which the Christian literally works out his or her salvation. Paul enjoins, 'Let him who stole steal no longer, but rather let him labour, working with his hands what is good, that he may have something to give him who has need' (Eph. 4:28).

In an increasingly secular world, when the majority have little or no gospel influence or contact with the Christian church, the main contact with Christians will be in the field of work – hence the necessity for a bright, attractive Christian testimony in the working hours. We are ambassadors for Christ! May we never bring reproach to His name or bring His cause into disrepute! While we cannot save a soul – only God can – it is surely our desire to show that faith 'works' and not to put any human stumbling block in the way of another person coming to Christ. Christians are not necessarily called to be successful, but they are called to be diligent, faithful, honest, cheerful and Christ-honouring in the place of work where God has put them – 'not with eyeservice, as men-pleasers, but in sincerity of heart, fearing God. And whatever you do, do it heartily, as to the Lord and not to men' (Col. 3:22, 23). Paul bids slaves – and by implication employees – 'to be well pleasing in all things … showing all good fidelity, that they may adorn the doctrine of God our Saviour in all things' (Titus 2:9, 10). Paul is exhorting us to make our salvation look attractive. Salvation is the greatest gift we can ever receive. We know it and we are to show it – to show it when 'the rubber grips the road' in the day-to-day, nitty-gritty of a wet Wednesday morning at work.

'The labourer is worthy of his hire.' We need to work, just as our work needs us. It is an unhappy situation if we should find ourselves unemployed. Yet work itself in a fallen world will never be without its stresses and strains. In the age to come, though, if we belong to Jesus, our work will be characterized by unending, unalloyed joy. The redeemed in glory 'are before the throne of God, and serve Him day and night in His temple' (Rev. 7:15). Currently, we work for a wage – and trust that we are 'worthy of our hire'. Then, our wage and reward will be the work itself – the joy of serving God without weariness or handicap. For only then will we fulfil our true end of 'glorifying God and enjoying Him for ever.'[1]

---

1. (See *The Westminster Shorter Catechism,* Question 1.)

9

The patience of Job

'She must have the patience of Job.' This expression is usually used admiringly, as a compliment. We use the expression 'the patience of Job' to describe someone who exercises 'putting-upmanship' – that is, someone who copes with difficult circumstances or with an irritating person without complaining, and continues to plough on in the path of duty in spite of the difficulties, discouragements and distractions.

Our expression under consideration is taken from the New Testament – though it refers to a character from Old Testament times. In James 5:11 we read, 'Behold, we count them happy which endure. Ye have heard of the patience of Job, and have seen the end of the Lord; that the Lord is very pitiful, and of tender mercy' (KJV).

The strange thing is, if we read the story of Job in the Old Testament, we see that Job does not always come across as a patient man. He suffered dreadfully and was driven to despair and exasperation by his losses, the well-meaning but incorrect pronouncements of his friends and, above all, with the incomprehensible, providential working of God in his life. In his excruciating suffering, 'Job opened his mouth and cursed the day of his birth' (Job 3:1). So Job was not exactly patient all the time …

James 5:11, however, does not really employ the word 'patience'. Under the guidance of the Holy Spirit, the Greek word James uses is the word '*hupomone*'. A better translation of this would be along the lines of 'steadfastness, perseverance, staying power'. Job certainly suffered. And he acted and reacted in a very human way to this – but he never lost his faith in God. This is the true meaning of the expression 'the patience of Job'.

'If we learn to persevere, even in the face of the incomprehensible ways of God in our lives, we have learnt the supreme lesson of the Book of Job. That lesson is to stick close to God through adversity and pain, no matter what.'[1]

The Background

The forty-two chapters of the Book of Job are set in the time of the Patriarchs, some two thousand years B.C. It is thus one of the oldest books in the world. Job is described in the opening verse as 'blameless and upright, and one who feared God and shunned evil' (Job 1:1). When we first meet Job, we see that he lived a happy and prosperous life. He enjoyed good health, a happy family life with his wife and children, and much material prosperity. Almost overnight, though, because of the evil intentions of Satan and the permissive, higher will of God, he lost it all. His possessions were destroyed, he was bereaved of his children and struck with a painful, disfiguring disease.

Job's initial reaction to his suffering and plight – submission to whatever God sees fit to send – is a model for everyone. He continued to worship God! He said, 'Naked I came from my mother's womb, and naked shall I return there. The LORD gave, and the LORD has taken away; blessed by the name of the LORD' (Job 1:21).

As Job's physical and mental suffering continued without any alleviation, three friends of his – 'miserable comforters' as it turned out – came and advised him. They tried to make sense of his suffering. The popular wisdom of the day taught them that

---

1. Derek Thomas, *The Storm Breaks: Job Simply Explained,* Evangelical Press (Darlington, 2003), p.16.

those who please God prosper in the world, while those who displease Him suffer adversity. It thus followed – by their logic – that Job had sinned. This general rule, though, did not fit Job's case. It was a misdiagnosis. And so they argued back and forth …

Eventually – after much arguing in circles – Almighty God Himself spoke. He gave Job a vision of His greatness, glory and infinite wisdom. Job's many questions about his plight were then answered by not being answered! He knew that God was God and held all the answers, doing all things well, present suffering notwithstanding. The message of Job is thus to trust God even when we do not understand what He is doing in our lives. We may not understand, but we can be sure He does. 'Then Job answered the LORD: "I know that thou canst do all things, and that no purpose of thine can be thwarted"' (Job 42:1, 2, RSV). The Book of Job ends happily, for 'The LORD restored Job's losses' (Job 42:10). His health was restored and God gave him double for all he had lost.

Encouragement from Job

The Book of Job contains many 'gems' to encourage us, and help us to praise God through 'thick and thin', whatever our circumstances. 'The LORD gave, and the LORD has taken away; Blessed be the name of the LORD' (Job 1:21).

> *Ye saints, who toil below,*
> *Adore your heavenly King,*
> *And onward as ye go*
> *Some joyful anthem sing;*
> *Take what He gives*
> *And praise Him still,*
> *Through good or ill,*
> *Who ever lives!*

> (RICHARD BAXTER, 1615–91)

Satan accused Job before God, suggesting that Job only served God because it was in his own interests to do so. It paid him. The truth, though, was otherwise. Job was steadfast in his conviction: 'Though He slay me, yet will I trust in Him' (Job 13:15, KJV).

Job was understandably perplexed as to God's 'strange' dealings with him. He did not know the reason for what was going on. But he knew that God knew. And we can have the same attitude when we experience God's darker providential dealings with us, and affirm, 'But He knows the way that I take; when He has tested me, I shall come forth as gold' (Job 23:10).

The message of Job – and the answer to the age-old dilemma of the apparent contradiction between the love and sovereignty of God and how this squares with human suffering – is that of persevering faith. God is on the throne. He is all-wise. He is all-loving. And we know He is all-loving, not because of our circumstances, but because we stand this side of the cross and the empty tomb. 'God demonstrates His own love toward us, in that while we were still sinners, Christ died for us' (Rom. 5:8). Jesus suffered for us, so that one day we will know no more suffering. With Job, we, too, can confess, 'I know that my Redeemer lives' (Job 19:25). God is trustworthy. We need to trust Him more than we do.

'The patience of Job'. Job was not particularly patient, but he persevered. He walked by faith. He trusted God. Job would have loved the hymn by an author of a different era, but one who also knew suffering and God's stranger providences in his life. The hymn goes like this:

> *God moves in a mysterious way*
> *His wonders to perform;*
> *He plants His footsteps in the sea*
> *And rides upon the storm.*

The patience of Job

Deep in unfathomable mines
Of never-failing skill,
He treasures up His bright designs
And works His sovereign will.

Judge not the Lord by feeble sense,
But trust Him for His grace;
Behind a frowning providence
He hides a smiling face!

His purposes will ripen fast,
Unfolding every hour;
The bud may have a bitter taste,
But sweet will be the flower.

(WILLIAM COWPER, 1731–1800)

10
'He's seen the light'

We use the expression 'to see the light' when people come to an understanding of a particular matter. They might be confused or ignorant about something, and so we explain it to them. Understanding dawns on them, and they exclaim 'Ah ha! I see it now.' They have seen the light … We are not referring to a physical light here, but rather to the light of understanding – not so much sight, but insight. One of the main rewards of teaching is when, through our explanation, understanding comes to a pupil or student and 'the penny drops'. The fact that they have grasped what you are explaining may be seen on their faces. They've got it! The light has dawned.

The Conversion of Paul

The expression 'He's seen the light' comes from the account of the conversion of Saul of Tarsus – the Apostle Paul – in the Bible. Paul's conversion to Christ on the road to Damascus has been termed the most momentous event in history after the death and resurrection of the Lord Jesus Christ. The account of Paul's conversion is related to us three times in the Book of Acts, and alluded to many more times in Paul's letters. Luke, the historian and medical doctor, records 'as he [that is, Paul] journeyed he came near Damascus, and suddenly a light shone around him from heaven. Then he fell to the ground, and heard a voice saying to him, "Saul, Saul, why are you persecuting Me? … I am Jesus, whom you are persecuting …"' (Acts 9:3-5).

Paul was never the same after that day. On the Damascus road, the light of salvation came to him. He was converted. He had a saving encounter with the crucified, risen, ascended and glorified Christ Himself. The ardent persecutor of the church now became an ardent preacher of Christ. Christianity's great opponent was to become Christianity's greatest exponent. Under God, the world is in debt to the Apostle Paul more than to any other human being. His epistle to the Romans, for instance, is the clearest, most reasoned exposition of the Christian faith ever penned. It was Paul's epistle to the Romans which sparked the Protestant Reformation with its rediscovery of the central message of the Bible, that salvation is by grace alone through faith alone in the crucified Christ alone.

On the Damascus road, therefore, Paul was converted. He 'saw the light'. Later on in his life, Paul testified before King Agrippa how 'I journeyed to Damascus … at midday, O king, along the road I saw a light from heaven, brighter than the sun, shining around me …' (Acts 26:12, 13). Jesus Himself proclaimed, 'I am the light of the world. He who follows Me shall not walk in darkness, but have the light of life' (John 8:12).

Christian Conversion

We may safely say that spectacular conversions like Paul's are not God's normal way of operating. Yet salvation today is still a matter of 'seeing the light'. By God's grace, we come to an understanding of ourselves as sinners under His judgment, and then see the provision He has made for sinners in the death of His Son, and are enabled to trust Him for our eternal salvation. Paul's salvation came to him on the Damascus road. God is free to work our salvation as He wills. It might be through our reading the Bible or hearing the gospel proclaimed in a church service, over the radio waves or in the open air – 'The Spirit of God maketh the reading, but especially the preaching of the Word, an effectual means of convincing and converting sinners, and of building them up in holiness and comfort, through faith, unto salvation' (*The Westminster Shorter Catechism,* answer to question 89). It might be through a gospel tract; it might be through the testimony of a Christian friend; perhaps some terrible tragedy, or some wonderful triumph may also be instrumental in leading us to Christ … The way God brings us to salvation varies. But everyone who has ever been saved has this in common: Like Paul, that person has a saving encounter with the Lord Jesus Christ and 'sees the light'. 'For it is the God who commanded light to shine out of darkness who has shone in our hearts to give the light of the knowledge of the glory of God in the face of Jesus Christ' (2 Cor. 4:6).

In the dark

Sadly, the Bible diagnoses all non-Christians as being in a state of spiritual darkness – dark as to their true condition, dark as to their need of a Saviour and dark as to their eternal destiny. Apart from a saving encounter with Christ, an even worse darkness of eternal hell awaits, for if we die without Christ, we die in an unforgiven state. Paul describes those who are out of Christ as 'having their understanding darkened, being alienated from the life of God, because of the ignorance that is in them, because of the blindness of their heart' (Eph. 4:18).

Salvation, therefore, is a matter of seeing the light. In Paul's epistle to the Ephesians, he also wrote, 'For you were once darkness, but now you are light in the Lord …' (Eph. 5:8). Paul's friend Peter could also likewise write to Christians saying that God has 'called you out of darkness into His marvellous light' (1 Pet. 2:9). Christians have seen the light!

The imperative, evangelistic question, therefore, is, 'Have *you* seen the light?' Do you know the Christ who is the light of the

47

world? The world today is generally steeped in darkness. Men and women without Christ live in the darkness of sin and under the wrath of God. But when we hear the gospel and believe, this darkness of our hearts and souls is banished by the light of Christ. 'Arise, shine; for your light has come! And the glory of the LORD is risen upon you. For behold, the darkness shall cover the earth, and deep darkness the people; but the LORD will arise over you, and His glory will be seen upon you' (Isa. 60:1, 2).

Christians have the light of Christ, and Christians will bask in the light of Christ for all eternity, for in the age to come 'there shall be no night there: they need no lamp nor light of the sun, for the Lord God gives them light. And they shall reign forever and ever' (Rev. 22:5).

Christians have seen the light!

> *I heard the voice of Jesus say,*
> *'I am this dark world's Light;*
> *Look unto Me, thy morn shall rise,*
> *And all thy day be bright!'*
> *I looked to Jesus, and I found*
> *In Him my Star, my Sun!*
> *And in that Light of life I'll walk,*
> *Till trav'ling days are done.*

(HORATIUS BONAR, 1808–89)

11

Head and shoulders above the rest

'He stands head and shoulders above the rest.' This popular expression is used in both a literal and a metaphorical way. Literally, it describes a person who is physically taller than average. When I was in primary school, there was a boy in the year above me who was freakishly tall. He was over six feet in height by the time he was nine years old. He was the goalkeeper for the school football team and could touch the crossbar with ease. In school assemblies he stood out 'head and shoulders above the rest'.

Metaphorically, our expression describes a person of outstanding character and ability. Recent history would perhaps suggest Sir Winston Churchill as a 'standout' character for his able and inspirational leadership of Great Britain during the Second World War. Then there is Muhammad Ali, once the heavyweight champion of the world. Although currently struggling with ill health, he must be one of the most recognizable men on the planet, with a charisma and personality that transcended the sport of boxing. These two men surely 'stand out head and shoulders above the rest'.

King Saul

The expression 'head and shoulders above the rest' has its origin in the Bible, during the transitional time in Israel's history, when the nation changed from being ruled by judges to being ruled by a king. Israel's first earthly king was a man by the name of Saul, and 1 Samuel 9:2 makes the point that Saul stood 'head and shoulders' above his contemporaries. 'There was not a more handsome person than he among the children of Israel. From his shoulders upward he was taller than any of the people.' Sadly, sacred history reveals that Saul's spiritual stature did not match his physical stature. First Samuel 13:8-14 relates his usurping the office of a priest. First Samuel 28 describes his seeking the help of a spirit medium. Both were contrary to the will of God. The Lord God eventually rejected Saul as a king and chose David in his place. First Samuel 31 records how Saul committed suicide and literally 'fell on his sword'. The question as to whether Saul was a true believer in God has been a matter of debate.

Christians

'He stands out head and shoulders above the rest.' In a spiritual sense, Christians are called to do just this. In a non-Christian world, we are called to stand out, because we are called to be holy. 'But as He who called you is holy, you also be holy in all your conduct, because it is written, "Be holy, for I am holy"' (1 Pet. 1:15, 16). To be holy is to stand out – to be different, separate and special. Technically, the word means 'to be set apart by God for God.' As only God Himself is truly holy, Christian holiness is by association. Christian holiness is not an intrinsic holiness but a derived one – derived from the Christian's faith union with Christ.

By way of illustration, the fourth commandment states 'Remember the Sabbath day, to keep it holy' (Exod. 20:8). The Sabbath Day – now our Sunday – is different from other days. This is the day when Christ rose from the dead. This is the day devoted specifically to God in the public and private exercises of divine worship. Sundays are special and different. They are 'holy days'. Similarly, Christians are special and different. Why? Because of divine grace. We are 'elect according to the foreknowledge of God the Father, in sanctification of the Spirit, for obedience and sprinkling of the blood of Jesus Christ' (1 Pet. 1:2). Christians are called to live a life of devotion to God, in response to His saving grace to us. We claim to be the objects of His special, saving favour – but do our lives in the secular world give evidence that this is, indeed, the case? In a sordid world, do we stand out for our purity of speech and character? In an age when disrespect, hatred, sexual impropriety, stealing, lying and greed abound, are we known to be different? Have we a zeal for keeping God's commandments? In a secular world, are we known as belonging to Jesus?

The word which encapsulates the holy quality of Christians is the word 'sanctification'. 'For this is the will of God, your sanctification …' (1 Thess. 4:3).

> *Sanctification is the work of God's free grace, whereby we are renewed in the whole man after the image of God and are enabled more and more to die unto sin and live unto righteousness.*[1]

In a nutshell, sanctification means that we become more and more like Jesus. This, of course, is not an instant but a gradual process. Thankfully, God does not leave us to our own devices but 'has also given us His Holy Spirit' (1 Thess. 4:8). The presence of the Holy Spirit within us can alone make us truly holy – producing in our lives the Christlike fruit of 'love, joy peace, longsuffering, kindness, goodness, faithfulness, gentleness, self-control' (Gal. 5:22, 23). Yes, it can be discouraging. Our growth in holiness can seem a matter of fits and starts. But take heart. God has not finished with His children yet! Pray, therefore, 'Lord, make me as holy as it is possible for a saved sinner to be.' Seek the aid of

---

1. *The Westminster Shorter Catechism,* Question 35

God's Holy Spirit to become more like Jesus. Be much in prayer and the reading of God's Word. Pilgrims should make progress, and pilgrims will, with God's help, make progress – 'being transformed into the same image [of Jesus] from glory to glory, just as by the Spirit of the Lord' (2 Cor. 3:18).

> *More holiness give me, more strivings within,*
> *More patience in suffering, more sorrow for sin;*
> *More faith in my Saviour, more sense of His care,*
> *More joy in His service, more purpose in prayer.*
>
> *More gratitude give me, more trust in the Lord,*
> *More zeal for His glory, more hope in His Word;*
> *More tears for His sorrows, more pain at His grief,*
> *More meekness in trial, more praise for relief.*
>
> *More purity give me, more strength to o'ercome,*
> *More freedom from earth-stains, more longings for home;*
> *More fit for the kingdom, more useful I'd be,*
> *More blessèd and holy, more, Saviour, like Thee.*

(PHILIP P BLISS, 1838–75)

Focus on Christ

Christians, therefore, are called to 'stand out head and shoulders above the rest' – to shine for the glory of God. Yet, when all is said and done, 'The best of men are men at best.' King Saul 'was taller than any of the people from his shoulders upward' (1 Sam. 10:23). He stood out physically, but sacred history reveals his faults, flaws and failings – as it does with many of the other personalities we encounter in the Bible. And is it not the same with us all? Truth be told, we are all sinners. Truth be told, history knows of just one truly outstanding man – a Man in a category all of His own, who towers above all the rest. We refer to the sinless Son of God Himself, the Lord Jesus Christ. He is truly beyond compare as He is no ordinary man. 'For in Him dwells all the fullness of the Godhead bodily' (Col. 2:9). While it

52

is incumbent on all Christians to 'stand out' for the glory of God, and seek to be the best we can for Him, the goal of the Christian faith ultimately is not to draw attention to ourselves as outstanding Christians but to bring honour and glory to Christ – to exalt Him in all the incomparable wonder of His person and all the outstanding glory of His redeeming work. There is truly none like Jesus. He stands out for more than head and shoulders above the rest. 'For in Him dwells all the fullness of the Godhead bodily; and you are complete in Him, who is the head of all principality and power' (Col. 2:9, 10).

12

A drop in the ocean

We use the expression 'It's just a drop in the ocean' sometimes in exasperation. It can describe what we perceive as our feeble and even futile efforts to change things. It is an expression we use in relation to our limitations. A charity collector on the street encourages us to give to help alleviate poverty in the developing world. We duly put a few pounds or dollars into a collection tin – but at the back of our minds we fear that our contribution is 'just a drop in the ocean'. Will it make any difference at all? We know that we lack the resources to solve Third-World poverty. What difference will our meagre contribution make?

Explanation

The exact expression 'a drop in the ocean' is not used in the Bible, but a similar expression is. The biblical expression is used to illustrate something of the unsurpassed and absolute, awesome greatness of Almighty God – and to fuel our faith and further our confidence in Him. The expression is to be found in Isaiah 40:15.

When Isaiah prophesied, the people of Israel were surrounded by hostile nations who threatened to conquer them. It is understandable that this caused the people of God to fear and their faith to waver. Isaiah's response, under God, was to remind the people as to just who their God is, and to keep their focus solely and squarely on Him. 'Say to the cities of Judah, "Behold your God!"' (Isa. 40:9). *He* is the One in sovereign control, not the rulers of the earth. In fact, Isaiah states, Almighty God is so incredibly great, that the nations of the world, though mighty, are insignificant in comparison. And so, coming to our expression, in Isaiah 40:15 we read 'Behold, the nations are as a drop in a bucket, and are counted as the small dust on the scales; Look, He lifts up the isles as a very little thing.' Isaiah then continues, saying that, in the sight of God 'All nations before Him are as nothing, and they are counted by Him less than nothing and worthless' (Isa. 40:17).

Yes, the nations were mighty, but the God of Israel alone – the living and true God – may be truly described as All-mighty. He is in sovereign control, states Isaiah, for He is the God of both creation and providence. He made the universe and He superintends the universe, working and weaving all things out according to His will and for His glory. 'It is He who sits above the circle of the earth, and its inhabitants are like grasshoppers, who stretches out the heavens like a curtain, and spreads them out like a tent to dwell in. He brings the princes to nothing; He makes the judges of the earth useless' (Isa. 40:22, 23).

'Behold, the nations are as a drop in a bucket …' in compari-son with Almighty God. If you were to fill a large bucket with water, and then drop a small drop of blue ink into it from a fountain pen, you would soon find that the blue ink disappears – it is absorbed by the great volume of water. Such are the nations of the world in relation to God, says our verse in Isaiah 40:15 – and, by impli-cation, such are our problems and difficulties in relation to Him, too. In fact, the illustration of 'a drop in a bucket' is inadequate to illustrate God's omnipotent greatness, for Isaiah also reminds us that Almighty God is far greater than even the vast oceans of the world, for He created these. His greatness is such that He could drown the oceans. His greatness is such that He could dwarf the highest of earthly mountains. Isaiah asks the rhetorical question of Almighty God: 'Who has measured the waters in the hollow of

His hand, measured heaven with a span and calculated the dust of the earth in a measure? Weighed the mountains in scales and the hills in a balance?' (Isa. 40:12).

Application

So whatever our problems, difficulties and troubles may be, the expression 'a drop in a bucket' reminds us that our God is greater than them all, and the resources of His saving and sustaining grace are more than adequate for His children's needs. Our view of God must be taken from the revelation He has given of Himself in the Bible. Anything less is idolatry. Idolatry involves thinking thoughts about God which are either false or unworthy of Him. *The Westminster Shorter Catechism* asks the question 'What is God?' Its matchless answer – fully in line with the doctrine of the Bible – goes:

> *God is a Spirit, infinite, eternal and unchangeable in His being, wisdom, power, holiness, justice, goodness and truth.*[1]

Such is the God of the Bible – the God and Father of our Lord Jesus Christ. And if we belong to Jesus, such is our God and Father. He is the greatest and best of all beings – omnipotent, omniscient and omnipresent. He is not subject to our limitations. Our large problems are small to Him. Our difficulties are easy for Him – just 'a drop in a bucket'. Take them to the Lord in prayer! Surely, if our troubles, difficulties and inadequacies drive us to Him and prove His total adequacy, they are actually blessings in disguise.

---

1. *The Westminster Shorter Catechism,* Question 4

13
A thorn in the flesh

When we use the expression 'a thorn in the flesh', we are referring to some physical ailment or troublesome person or circumstance which makes our life hard, difficult and unpleasant. 'My
osteoarthritis is a thorn in the flesh. I've had to give up playing
squash.' 'X in my office is a thorn in the flesh. He always seems
to be out to make life awkward for me.' Our 'thorn in the flesh' –
whatever it may be – is that which hinders and handicaps us from
living our lives as smoothly and easily as we would like.

The expression 'a thorn in the flesh' is another one which has
its origins in the Bible. In Old Testament times – during the eras
of Moses and Joshua – when the Israelites were about to enter
the promised land of Canaan, God ordered them to drive out the
inhabitants of the land. Canaanite practices were abominable to
God, and their worshipping of idols would be a temptation to the
Israelites if they were not destroyed – tempting them to turn away
from the one true God. So God gave the warning to His people: 'If
you do not drive out the inhabitants of the land from before you,
then it shall be that those whom you let remain shall be irritants in
your eyes and *thorns in your sides,* and they shall harass you in
the land where you dwell' (Num. 33:55, emphasis mine).

Paul's Painful Problem

Most notably, however, the expression 'a thorn in the flesh' was
used by the Apostle Paul in the New Testament to describe a
predicament in which he found himself. In 2 Corinthians 12:7,
Paul relates how, in the sovereign will of God, '*a thorn in the
flesh* was given to me, a messenger of Satan to buffet me ...'
(emphasis mine). The nature of this painful affliction is unspeci-

fied, and people have speculated on various conditions that Paul could have been referring to. Paul had just testified how once he had had a phenomenal blessing. He had actually been caught up into 'Paradise' – 'the third heaven' – and basked in the glorious presence of God Himself. It was indescribable. It could not have been better. But God brought him down to earth just to keep him 'grounded' on an even keel. Paul relates, 'And lest I should be exalted above measure by the abundance of the revelations, a thorn in the flesh was given to me, a messenger of Satan to buffet me, lest I be exalted above measure' (2 Cor. 12:7).

Amidst his pain, Paul then followed normal Christian practice. He prayed. So painful, weakening and debilitating was his affliction that he prayed to God to remove it. 'Concerning this thing I pleaded with the Lord three times that it might depart from me' (2 Cor. 12:8). And God answered Paul's prayer – but He answered it in His own, 'alternative' way. Instead of removing Paul's 'thorn', God gave Paul grace to live with it and bear it. Paul testified 'And He [God] said to me, "My grace is sufficient for you, for My strength is made perfect in weakness." Therefore most gladly I will rather boast in my infirmities, that the power of Christ may rest upon me' (2 Cor. 12:9). So Paul's weakened state magnified God's power. Paul's ministry could not be humanly explained. It was solely a result of God working in and through him. The weakness of the human instrument ensured that God received all the glory.

What, then, are the lessons we may learn from the painful experience of having 'a thorn in the flesh' – an experience we are all sure to have?

Expect them

First of all, we must expect to receive 'thorns in the flesh' of varying kinds. Ease is for heaven, not earth. Paul lived close to the Lord, but was not exempt from suffering. Neither are we. Jesus said, 'In the world you will have tribulation' (John 16:33). 'We must through many tribulations enter the kingdom of God' (Acts 14:22).

Blessings in disguise?

The 'thorns' that God sends our way are actually blessings in disguise. The God of infinite goodness can only send good things to His children. The problem is, our notion of 'goodness' may differ from His. He is the fount of every blessing. If 'thorns' drive us to Him, they certainly are blessings. Our inadequacy will prove His total adequacy. Paul testified early in 2 Corinthians 1:8, 9 'that we were burdened beyond measure, above strength, so that we despaired even of life. Yes, we had the sentence of death in ourselves, that we should not trust in ourselves but in God who raises the dead.'

The thorns of life knock away our self-sufficiency and enable us to realize afresh our total dependence on the saving and sustaining grace of God. Hence the Psalmist could say 'It is good for me that I have been afflicted, that I may learn Your statutes' (Ps. 119:71).

Prayer

Paul's example reveals that we are at liberty to pray to God to take our painful thorns away from us, if it is His will. 'Have we trials and temptations? Is there trouble anywhere? We should never be discouraged; take it to the Lord in prayer.'[1] Prayer is the Christian's inestimable privilege. Through Christ, we have an audience with heaven! Through Christ we have the ear of the Almighty.

---

1. Joseph M. Scriven, *What a Friend we have in Jesus,* 1855

Grace sufficient

If God does not see fit to 'extract' our particular thorn from us, we can say, on the authority of the Bible, that He will surely give us grace to live with it. God's promise to Paul is also God's promise to all His children: 'My grace is sufficient for you' (2 Cor. 12:9). As a man once said: 'I prayed to God for a lighter load. He answered my prayer by giving me a stronger back.' The Bible assures us that 'God is faithful, who will not allow you to be tempted [that is, tested] beyond what you are able, but with the temptation will also make the way of escape, that you may be able to bear it' (1 Cor. 10:13).

'A thorn in the flesh.' Thorns will surely come our way. But the Christian is assured that they are not haphazard events. Rather, they come from the gracious hand of God, who rules the world by His providence. He is well able to remove thorns from us – but He is equally able to enable us to live with them, to His glory.

> *He giveth more grace as the burdens grow greater,*
> *He sendeth more strength as the labours increase.*
> *To added afflictions He addeth His mercy,*
> *To multiplied trials, His multiplied peace.*
>
> *His love has no limits, His grace has no measure,*
> *His power has no boundary known unto men.*
> *For out of His infinite riches in Jesus,*
> *He giveth, and giveth, and giveth again!*

(ANNIE JOHNSON FLINT, 1866–1932)

14

A wolf in sheep's clothing

To describe someone as 'a wolf in sheep's clothing' is to refer to someone who, while appearing friendly, affable, honest and credible on the outside, is actually out to do us harm. The writer well remembers a time when a professing Christian asked him for the loan of a thousand pounds. The man was in tears as he related how he needed the money to send his daughter to America for a life-saving operation which could save her from her alleged cancer. Thankfully, before I parted with the money, I found out that the man was a total charlatan, and was well known for using various ploys to extort money from Christians – money which he never paid back. He was 'a wolf in sheep's clothing'. He was not what he seemed. But being such an expert at tugging at people's heartstrings, it was easy to be taken in by him.

The expression 'a wolf in sheep's clothing' stems from a warning given by the Lord Jesus in His famous 'Sermon on the Mount'. The warning He gave there was a warning against false prophets – religious leaders and teachers who might seem credible, but are not actually 'of God'. Such false prophets are like dangerous wolves, He said. They are highly harmful, for if a person is taken in by them, their false teaching, along with the false assurance of salvation they proclaim, is enough to damn a soul for all eternity. Jesus warned: 'Beware of false prophets, who come to you in sheep's clothing, but inwardly they are ravenous wolves' (Matt. 7:15).

It seems as though false prophets have always been around and will always be around until Christ comes again. In Jeremiah 23:16, God warned: 'Thus says the LORD of hosts: "Do not listen to the words of the prophets who prophesy to you. They make you worthless; they speak a vision of their own heart, not from the mouth of the LORD.'" And the Lord Jesus also taught that, before He returns in power and great glory, 'False christs and false prophets will rise and show great signs and wonders to deceive, if possible, even the elect' (Matt. 24:24).

To be forewarned is to be forearmed. The question is: How do we know whether the friendly person who knocks at our door wearing a suit and shiny shoes, handing out religious literature, is actually 'a wolf in sheep's clothing' or not? The touchstone for all religious truth – whether it is 'of God' or not – is: Does what is offered and proffered square with what God has revealed in His Word, the Bible? Do these teachers accept that the Bible is the inspired, inerrant Word of God and the final authority for all matters of faith and practice? Do they believe in the Trinitarian nature of the God revealed in the Bible? Do they believe that we are all sinners who need to be saved? Do they exalt the Lord Jesus as the eternal Son of God and the only Saviour, and preach that saving faith in Him in His atoning death is the only roadblock to hell? Do they preach that salvation is by divine grace alone – through the cross of Christ alone – that salvation is a result of what Christ has done, not what we do? Paul wrote, 'I do not set aside the grace of God; for if righteousness comes through the law, then Christ died in vain' (Gal. 2:21).

Jesus warned: 'Beware of false prophets, who come to you in sheep's clothing, but inwardly they are ravenous wolves' (Matt. 7:15). Sadly, the 'ravenous wolves' abound today. Here is a couple inviting you to take some of their literature – but they cannot be truly Christian, as they deny the deity of Christ, believing Him to be a created being and not eternal. Such a 'Christ' could not offer His life as an eternally atoning sacrifice for sin. Here is a clergyman. He is an affable bachelor and wears a clerical collar. He and his denomination preach and practise that salvation is gained through following various rituals prescribed by his church. Such is a denial of the all-sufficiency of Christ's sacrifice at Calvary. Such is a denial that salvation is 'the gift of God, not of works, lest anyone should boast' (Eph. 2:8, 9). Here is a man wearing non-Western clothing. His final authority is a book other than the Bible. His God is a God other than the God and Father of our Lord Jesus Christ. Though he recognizes Christ as a prophet, his religion is adamant that 'God has no son.' He urges you to follow his God. The Bible, however, teaches that the final revelation and full salvation of the one, true God is in Jesus Christ alone: 'Whoever denies the Son does not have the Father either; he who acknowledges the Son has the Father also' (1 John 2:23).

Jesus' warning to 'Beware of false prophets, who come to you in sheep's clothing, but inwardly they are ravenous wolves' seems, if anything, even more applicable today than at any other time in world history. How incumbent it is upon us to be well grounded in the truth of God's Word, so that we can easily detect the religious counterfeits that are around and flourishing. Peter was one with his Master when he wrote, 'But there were also false prophets among the people, even as there will be false teachers among you, who will secretly bring in destructive heresies, even denying the Lord who bought them …' (2 Pet. 2:1). John likewise enjoined: 'Beloved, do not believe every spirit, but test the spirits, whether they are of God; because many false prophets have gone out into the world. By this you know the Spirit of God: Every spirit that confesses that Jesus Christ has come in the flesh is of God, and every spirit that does not confess that Jesus Christ has come in the flesh is not of God …' (1 John 4:1-3).

At the heart of biblical Christianity is the Person and Work of the Lord Jesus Christ. Any religious person or organization which detracts from Him and His finished work of redemption is to be avoided at all costs. The people concerned may be sincere, and seem 'nice' – but they are actually 'wolves in sheep's clothing'. The false gospel they proclaim is eternally dangerous. If you are taken in by them, you are liable to spend eternity away from the light, love and life of the true and living God. Ensure then that your focus is 'Sola Christus' – Christ alone. All other ground is sinking sand. John Newton wrote:

What think you of Christ? is the test
To try both your state and your scheme;
You cannot be right in the rest,
Unless you think rightly of Him.
As Jesus appears in your view,
As He is beloved or not;
So God is disposed to you,
And mercy or wrath are your lot.

Some take Him a creature to be,
A man, or an angel at most;
Sure these have not feelings like me,
Nor know themselves wretched and lost:
So guilty, so helpless, am I,
I durst not confide in His blood,
Nor on His protection rely,
Unless I were sure He is God.

Some call Him a Saviour, in word,
But mix their own works with His plan;
And hope He His help will afford,
When they have done all that they can:
If doings prove rather too light
(A little, they own, they may fail)
They purpose to make up full weight,
By casting His name in the scale.

If asked what of Jesus I think?
Though still my best thoughts are but poor;
I say, He's my meat and my drink,
My life, and my strength, and my store,
My Shepherd, my Husband, my Friend,
My Saviour from sin and from thrall;
My hope from beginning to end,
My Portion, my Lord, and my All.

(JOHN NEWTON, 1725 -1807)

15

Be sure your sin will find you out

The above expression made the news headlines in the summer of 2011. A well-known Premiership footballer was allegedly having an 'affair' with a model – that is, sexual relations with someone who was not his wife. He paid for an expensive 'super-injunction' which prohibited the claims from being reported in the press. News leaked out, however, and his name was widely reported on the Internet. Then in the British Parliament his name was mentioned by an M.P. whose 'parliamentary privilege' was not subject to the super-injunction of the court. Thus the alleged 'secret affair' was no longer secret. He was publicly shamed. The phrase was often quoted: 'Be sure your sin will find you out.'

Back to the Bible

Few were aware that the expression 'Be sure your sin will find you out' is a biblical one, but it is. You will find it in Numbers 32:23. It was originally spoken by Moses. The context of the verse is this: The people of Israel were about to enter the Promised Land, west of the river Jordan. The tribes of Reuben and Gad, however, preferred to settle east of the Jordan, as the land there was favourable for their livestock. Moses was happy for them to stay there, but stipulated that, in the event of war, the tribes of Reuben and Gad must cross the Jordan and aid their brethren against their enemies. Moses warned, 'But if you do not do so, then take note, you have sinned against the LORD; and be sure your sin will find you out' (Num. 32:23). That verse, though, has a far wider application than solely its original one to the tribes of Reuben and Gad.

'Be sure your sin will find you out.' Sin can find us out. Adultery may wreck a marriage and family. Stealing may put us in jail. Lying on your CV could lose you your job … Yet reality suggests that sin does not always 'find us out'. There are unsolved murders. Some people live very opulently from the proceeds of crime. The tenth commandment prohibits covetousness – yet modern advertising is based on covetousness. The verse, however, holds true when we realize the true nature of sin.

Sin and its consequences

The Westminster Shorter Catechism defines sin as 'any want of conformity unto, or transgression of, the law of God'.[1] Sin will thus eventually find everybody out, as ultimately, sin is against God Himself, the holy and righteous Lawgiver. When we sin – and 'there is not a just man on earth who does good and does not sin' (Eccles. 7:20) – we break God's law and bring guilt on ourselves. 'For whoever shall keep the whole law, and yet stumble in one point, he is guilty of all' (James 2:10). As God is righteous, He cannot overlook the slightest infraction of His law. He has no option but to punish sinners. We might 'get away' with sin for a while, but only for a while. God knows our sin, for He is omniscient. We cannot hide from God. In the sight of God there is no such thing as a secret sin, for 'there is no creature hidden from His sight, but all things are naked and open to the eyes of Him to whom we must give account' (Heb. 4:13). When will God condemn us for our sins fully and finally? On the impending Judgment Day. This day is indelibly set on the divine

---

1. *The Westminster Shorter Catechism* , Question 14

calendar, as 'it is appointed for men to die once, but after this the judgment' (Heb. 9:27).

As we are all sinners – 'If we say that we have no sin, we deceive ourselves, and the truth is not in us' (1 John 1:8) – and as sin is so abhorrent to a holy God that He has no option but to punish sinners, is there any hope for us at all? Yes there is. There is a gospel of saving grace. The forgiveness of sins lies at the very heart of the Christian gospel, making it the good news that it is – making it 'music to the sinner's ear'.

Good news for condemned sinners

In His unfathomable love, God sent His Son into the world to save sinners. 'For God did not send His Son into the world to condemn the world, but that the world through Him might be saved' (John 3:17). 'Christ Jesus came into the world to save sinners' (1 Tim. 1:15).

If God did not punish sin, His righteousness would be compromised. But if God condemned all sinners to hell, the love which is at the heart of His nature would be compromised. In a sense, there was then – speaking reverently – a divine dilemma in the mind of God. This divine dilemma was solved in the wisdom of God by sending His Son to die in the place of sinners and bear the punishment they deserved. Because of the cross of Calvary, God is able both to punish sin and pardon the believing sinner – and therefore both to be just and a justifier. On the cross, God's own Son paid the penalty for our sins in our room and stead, so that by believing in Him we might know the forgiveness of sins. 'Christ died for our sins' (1 Cor. 15:3). '... who Himself bore our sins in His own body on the tree' (1 Pet. 2:24).

'Be sure your sin will find you out.' It's a formidable verse. Yet it is a verse that holds no terror for us if the saving grace of God

69

in Christ has also found us out. If we are Christians, we are not necessarily a good people, but we are a forgiven people – forgiven because Jesus has procured our forgiveness on Calvary's cross. 'In Him we have redemption through His blood, the forgiveness of sins, according to the riches of His grace' (Eph. 1:7).

The *Apostles' Creed* contains the line 'I believe … in the forgiveness of sins.' It does so with good reason, for the forgiveness of sins through the shedding of the precious blood of Jesus lies at the very heart of the Christian gospel. We never graduate beyond the cross of Calvary!

> *He died that we might be forgiven,*
> *He died to make us good,*
> *That we might go at last to heaven,*
> *Saved by His precious blood!*
>
> *There was no other good enough,*
> *To pay the price of sin.*
> *He only could unlock the gate,*
> *Of heaven and let us in.*

(MRS C. F. ALEXANDER, 1818–95)

16
O ye of little faith

The expression 'O ye of little faith' is often used as a retort to someone of a cynical, doubtful disposition. Standing on a railway platform, waiting for the train, we overhear someone say, 'These trains are always late' – but then the train arrives exactly on time. 'O you of little faith', quips a passenger to the cynic, as the train draws in. The expression has also been used in relation to the English cricket team. The English have somehow acquired the sporting reputation of being game but gallant losers. Not so long ago, however, the English cricket team actually won the Ashes against Australia. Such wins are a welcome boost to national morale. 'O ye of little faith', chortled one commentator after this English victory.

The words 'O ye of little faith' may be found verbatim in Luke 12:28 (KJV). They originate from the lips of the Lord Jesus Christ and are actually a gentle rebuke. The words were part of a discourse He gave to His disciples – and us – to encourage us to trust God to provide all that we need for our earthly welfare. Faith is only as good as its object, and God our Father – says the Lord Jesus – is infinitely trustworthy, and will never let His children down.

The Divine Antidote to Worry

The Lord Jesus knew only too well how prone we all are to anxiety. The antidote to worry, says the Saviour, is faith – or more specifically, faith in God – faith in the God revealed in the Bible. We, as Christians, are thus to be characterized as much by sustaining faith as we are by saving faith. We may entrust our earthly

71

welfare to God our Father, just as we have trusted Him for our eternal welfare. As we take up the Lord's discourse, and as we put this expression into context, we see just how well His words apply to us in a context in which we may be prone to anxiety.

'Therefore I say to you, do not worry about your life, what you will eat; nor about the body, what you will put on. Life is more than food, and the body is more than clothing. Consider the ravens, for they neither sow nor reap, which have neither storehouse nor barn; and God feeds them. Of how much more value are you than the birds? And which of you by worrying can add one cubit to his stature? If you then are not able to do the least, why are you anxious for the rest? Consider the lilies, how they grow: they neither toil nor spin; and yet I say to you, even Solomon in all his glory was not arrayed like one of these. If then God so clothes the grass, which today is in the field and tomorrow is thrown into the oven, how much more will He clothe you, *O you of little faith?*' (Luke 12:22 ff., emphasis mine).

The Master-Teacher is here arguing from the lesser to the greater: If God cares for flowers – which He does by clothing them – and if He cares for the birds of the air – which He does by feeding them – what of us? We are His special creatures, made in His image. We have been redeemed by the blood of His own Son. We have been adopted into God's family and so are able to call Him 'Abba, Father'. This being so, it is just unthinkable that God our Father will not care, provide and undertake for His children. Why worry, then? 'If God is for us, who can be against us?' (Rom. 8:31). 'He cares for you' (1 Pet. 5:7).

Worry is actually a sin. It casts aspersions on the character of God. It has the audacity to suggest that He is not good, and neither is He wise and able, nor in providential control over all things – the world in general, and His children's lives in particular.

We thus need to employ and apply the antidote of Jesus every time anxious thoughts arise, replacing them with faith in God. We have a Father in heaven! He loves us with an everlasting love. He is too wise to make mistakes and too loving to be unkind.

> *Said the robin to the sparrow,*
> *'I would really like to know*
> *why those anxious human beings*
> *rush around and worry so?'*
>
> *Said the sparrow to the robin,*
> *'Friend, I think that it must be*
> *they have no heavenly Father*
> *such as cares for you and me!'*
>
> (ANON.)

Strengthening our Faith

Scripture suggests that there are degrees of faith. In our expression, Jesus refers to 'little faith'. But in Matthew 15:28, He commends a Canaanite woman for her 'great faith'. Paul expressed delight in the Thessalonian Christians 'because your faith grows exceedingly' (2 Thess. 1:3). On another occasion, the disciples came to Jesus with the request, 'Increase our faith' (Luke 17:5). Wishing to avoid the Lord's rebuke of us for 'little faith', how do we 'increase our faith'?

Faith is actually a gift of God. Yet there are steps which we can take to increase our faith in God. He has provided the 'means of grace for us'. Two of these are:

The Scriptures

The Bible is God's own revelation of His character. The more we know the Bible, the better we will know God. And the better we know God, the more we will know of the infinite reliability, dependability and trustworthiness of His character. Memorizing and meditating on the promises of the Bible are ways in which our faith in God will grow. The Bible feeds our faith. 'The LORD is my rock and my fortress and my deliverer; my God, my strength, in whom I will trust; my shield and the horn of my salvation, my stronghold' (Ps. 18:2). How worthy He is of our trust! 'My God shall supply all your need according to His riches in glory by Christ Jesus' (Phil. 4:19).

Our Sufferings

In the Christian life, it is true that there is no gain without pain. In His wisdom and love, God sends suffering our way. Through this, our faith grows. In this, when our earthly props are taken away from us, we are cast more closely on God, and prove the all-sufficiency of His sustaining grace for our need. If God did not send us suffering, it is doubtful whether we would cultivate nearness to Him or see the need for it. Hence the Psalmist could testify, 'It is good for me that I have been afflicted, that I may learn Your statutes' (Ps. 119:71). It is in the University of Adversity that we learn the reliability of our God and that our faith in Him is increased. 'God is faithful' (1 Cor. 10:13). 'He never fails' (Zeph. 3:5).

Faith is only as good as its object. The Christian's faith is in a faithful God. Our faith will always be imperfect this side of eternity. Anxiety will arise. Hence, until our faith is turned to sight, we will always have to bear in mind our Saviour's gentle rebuke: 'O ye of little faith' – along with His all-embracing exhortation: 'Have faith in God' (Mark 11:22).

17

'A man after my own heart'

We use the expression 'He's a man after my own heart' to refer to someone who views the world in a way similar to ourselves, and has the desire to please us and make us happy. Here is a writer, writing at his desk. He has been there for over two hours. There is a knock on his study door and he is interrupted by a person holding a tray of tea and biscuits. Most welcome. 'Thank you. Just what is needed. You're a man after my own heart.'

King David

The expression 'He's a man after my own heart' actually originates from the mouth of Almighty God Himself. He used it to describe David, a shepherd from Bethlehem who was to become Israel's greatest king. Paul, quoting the Old Testament record in a sermon, related how God 'raised up for them David as king, to whom also He gave testimony and said, "I have found David the son of Jesse, *a man after My own heart,* who will do all My will"' (Acts 13:22, emphasis mine).

The biblical record reveals that David had many admirable qualities and abilities, and performed remarkable exploits. God had His hand on David's life. 'He also chose David His servant, and took him from the sheepfolds; from following the ewes that had young He brought him, to shepherd Jacob His people, and Israel His inheritance. So he shepherded them according to the integrity of his heart, and guided them by the skilfulness of his hands' (Ps. 78:70-72).

David was a shepherd, musician, poet, warrior, father, politician and king. He had 'charisma'. He eventually united the whole of Israel under his monarchy, and gave her a degree of peace and stability, having overcome her enemies and established Jerusalem as her religious and political capital. The people of Israel looked back on David's era as something of a golden age.

Above all, however, David was a man of God. Samuel said to Saul of David: 'The LORD has sought for Himself *a man after His own heart,* and the LORD has commanded him to be commander over His people …' (1 Sam. 13:14, emphasis mine). The intimate relationship which David had with God Himself is evident especially from the many psalms which David composed. In Psalm 18:1, 2, for instance, David confesses: 'I will love You, O LORD, my strength. The LORD is my rock and my fortress and my deliverer; my God, my strength, in whom I will trust; my shield and the horn of my salvation, my stronghold.'

You and I?

Being described as 'a man after God's own heart' is surely the highest accolade of all. Can you and I ever hope to be described as the same? Amazingly, by God's grace, we can, for through the Lord Jesus Christ and His death on the cross we may attain both reconciliation and intimacy with God Himself. Then, through reading His Word, we may find out what pleases God and seek to do and obey the same. The Bible is the revelation of God's own mind and will. It is the heart and mind of God in print. With the aid of God's Word and His promised Spirit within us, therefore, we may be gradually changed – and even transformed – more and more into the people God would have us be – no less than people after His own heart.

Perfectly imperfect

David was, indeed, 'a man after God's own heart'. The Bible tells us so. Yet paradoxically, the biblical record also reveals that David was far from sinless. There were times when he displeased God as well as those when he pleased Him. Perhaps most notoriously of all, David broke God's seventh commandment when he committed adultery with Bathsheba. Then, in 2 Samuel 24, another of David's lapses is recorded. He numbered the people, putting his faith in military might rather than in God Himself. On both occasions, David suffered the consequences of his actions. Did these occasions nullify his being 'a man after God's own heart' though? No, because whenever David sinned, he turned back to God. He repented. He begged for mercy, forgiveness and the restoration of fellowship. And he sought divine help to amend his ways and please God in the future. Psalm 51 is David's eloquent testimony to his sincere repentance after his adultery with Bathsheba. It is a prayer we will do well to make our own when we have spoiled our conscious enjoyment of fellowship with God. Sadly, Christians still sin because we are still sinners by nature. This will be our story until the age to come when we will be saved to sin no more. But the difference between a Christian and a non-Christian – one who is a 'man after God's own heart' and one who is not – is in the reaction to our sinning. A true Christian will be characterized by a life of repentance – a continual turning and returning to God for mercy, forgiveness and restoration, and a desire to please God as much as is possible for a saved sinner to do so. The Apostle John was one of Christ's intimate friends. But even as a mature Christian, he wrote: 'If we say that we have no sin, we deceive ourselves, and the truth is not in us. If we confess our sins, He is faithful and just to forgive us our sins and to cleanse us from all unrighteousness' (1 John 1:8, 9). Confession is good for the soul!

King Jesus

David was 'a man after God's own heart' – yet he was so imperfectly. The true 'man after God's own heart' was the Lord Jesus Christ, God's Son – 'Great David's Greater Son'. At His baptism, 'a voice came from heaven, "You are My beloved Son, in whom I am well pleased"' (Mark 1:11). Of all the children of men, Jesus alone could make the claim, 'I always do those things that please Him' (John 8:29). David had his moments of rebellion against, and disobedience to, the will of God. The Lord Jesus, however, obeyed the will and law of God perfectly. Putting words into His mouth, the Psalmist wrote prophetically of Him: 'Then I said, "Behold, I come; in the scroll of the book it is written of me. I delight to do Your will, O my God, and Your law is within my heart"' (Ps. 40:7, 8). Before His death at Calvary, Christ prayed to His Father: 'Not as I will, but as You will' (Matt. 26:39). 'He … became obedient to the point of death, even the death of the cross' (Phil. 2:8).

It is both the active and the passive obedience of the Lord Jesus Christ which takes us to the heart of the gospel. He was truly 'a man after God's own heart'. He came to do God's will of accomplishing the eternal salvation of His people. He lived a sinless life, fulfilling God's law to the letter. Then He died in the place of His people, bearing their punishment and paying their penalty for breaking God's law. Undeniably, Jesus was 'a man after God's own heart'! And through faith in Him, sinners enter into all the benefits and blessings which His active and passive obedience achieved, and are reconciled to God for time and eternity. Salvation, according to the Bible, is achieved not by our merits but by the merits of Another – the Lord Jesus Christ, the King of kings and Lord of lords, the true 'Man after God's own heart'.

18

To give up the ghost

The term 'to give up the ghost' is sometimes used when, for example, something has broken or when someone has given up trying. An example of the first would be 'We've got to get a new TV, as our old one has finally given up the ghost.' An example of the second one would be 'Poor Tom. He's been trying to get his novel published. After twelve rejections from various publishers, though, he's finally given up the ghost.'

The expression 'to give up the ghost' is another example of the way the King James Bible has permeated our English language. In the Bible, though, the expression is used in a rather different way from the way it is popularly used today. The expression actually originates from the most momentous time in world history, for the Gospel writers employ it in their reporting of the death of the Lord Jesus at Calvary. Luke records the final minutes of Jesus' life, when He hung on the cross for the redemption of His people: 'when Jesus had cried with a loud voice, He said, "Father, into Thy hands I commend my spirit": and having said thus, *He gave up the ghost'* (Luke 23:46, KJV, emphasis mine). John's account complements Luke's. John notes that Jesus' loud cry was not a cry of defeat but a cry of triumph. Jesus cried words as if to say, 'I have accomplished the salvation of my people, Father. I have finished the work You gave me to do.' 'He said "It is finished": and He bowed His head, and *gave up the ghost'* (John 19:30, KJV, emphasis mine).

What, though, do we learn from the Saviour's 'giving up the ghost'?

Unique Sonship

Jesus' first and last recorded words were the word 'Father'. As a twelve-year-old boy, His first recorded words were uttered in the temple at Jerusalem, when He explained, 'Did you not know that I must be about My Father's business?' (Luke 2:49). Whereas among His last recorded words, just before He died, were, 'Father, into Your hands I commend My spirit' (Luke 23:46). This reminds us of Jesus' unique identity. He Himself was aware of His unique relationship to the Father – His unique sonship. While Christians become the sons of God through Christ – adoption is one of the Bible's synonyms for salvation – Jesus' divine sonship was intrinsic and eternal. He is the unique – the 'only-begotten' Son of God – 'begotten not made, being of one substance with the Father' (*Nicene Creed*). While we become the sons of God when we believe in Jesus, Jesus always was the Son of God. He existed in eternity past in the unity of love which exists in the one God who is revealed in Scripture as the divine trinity of God the Father, God the Son and God the Holy Spirit.

Total Sovereignty

On Calvary, Jesus 'gave up the ghost'. He was in total control. The Bible is adamant that Jesus' life was not taken *from* Him, but given *by* Him. Jesus Himself once explained, 'I lay down My life that I may take it again. No one takes it from Me, but I lay it down of Myself. I have power to lay it down, and I have power to take it again …' (John 10:17, 18). Paul often reiterated this teaching of the Lord: 'the Son of God, who loved me and gave Himself for me' (Gal. 2:20). 'Christ also has loved us and given Himself for us, an offering and a sacrifice to God' (Eph. 5:2). Christ 'gave Himself for us, that He might redeem us from every lawless deed and purify for Himself His own special people …' (Titus 2:14). So Christ's life was not taken from Him, but given by Him. In the eternal plan of God, He willingly gave Himself as an atoning sacrifice for sinners.

Peaceful Serenity

Having procured the eternal salvation of His people by dying in their place and paying the penalty for their sins, Jesus entrusted His soul to God the Father and 'gave up the ghost'. At the dawn of history, God the Father rested on the seventh day, having completed the work of creation. Having completed the work of redemption, God the Son's body was laid to rest in the tomb of Joseph of Arimathea. His soul, though, went back to His Father in Paradise, before being reunited with His body on the first day of the week – the glorious resurrection morning.

When we read the account of Jesus' final moments, we are struck by the note of peaceful serenity. Death ultimately had no terrors for Him. He entrusted His soul to God the Father and 'gave up the ghost'. Death holds no terrors for all who belong to Jesus too, for Jesus has taken the sting of death away, and Jesus has blazed a trail into the Father's presence for us. Because of the death of Jesus, for Christians, death itself will be merely the porter who ushers us into Paradise – into the nearer presence of God Himself. And we, too, are promised that one day we will be reunited to our bodies, and raised to immortality – a new, more glorious existence. Christ has opened Paradise for us. Christ has paved the way for us. Christ has set the pattern for us. The true Christian's hope – that is, confident expectation – is not only the salvation of the soul but the resurrection of the body. Jesus will come again and 'transform our lowly body that it may be conformed to His glorious body' (Phil. 3:21). 'The trumpet will sound, and the dead will be raised incorruptible, and we shall be changed' (1 Cor. 15:52).

Giving up the ghost

So the origins of the expression 'giving up the ghost' have nothing to do with broken TVs or frustrated plans. The expression takes us back to the cross of Calvary which is the very heart of the Christian faith. It reminds us of Jesus' unique identity – He is the only Son of God. It reminds us of His absolute sovereignty – He gave His life to ransom us. It assures us that death holds no terror for those who belong to Jesus, and makes us look ahead to the glorious future which is the new birthright of every believer. We anticipate worshipping God in redeemed bodies in a redeemed universe. For the Christian, the best is yet to be!

19

'Don't judge by appearances!'

The popular expression 'Don't judge by appearances' can sometimes seem a little harsh, as appearances are often all we have to go on. Appearances, though, can deceive. The writer remembers how in the washroom on his first day at college, he encountered a little, rather podgy man, wearing shorts and open-toed sandals. Three days later, he found out that this short, fat man in shorts and sandals was actually the professor of the whole faculty! We are also sometimes enjoined, 'Don't judge a book by its cover.' It is, of course, the contents of a book which give it its lasting worth or otherwise. Yet if there were no value in a book's cover at all, why do publishers go to such lengths to make the cover attractive to the eye and its back-cover text striking to the person who may peruse it? The outer cover of a book is the first thing we notice when browsing in a book store. It is the 'bait' which might make us investigate and purchase it.

The actual expression 'Don't judge by appearances' is not found verbatim in the Bible, but the thought and spirit of the expression is definitely there. In 1 Samuel 16:7, we read, 'But the LORD said to Samuel, "Do not look at his appearance or at his physical stature, because I have refused him. For the LORD does not see as man sees; for man looks at the outward appearance, but the LORD looks at the heart."' This verse teaches us that the all-seeing God looks beyond the cosmetic and outward veneer. He sees the real 'you'. He knows what we are really like.

Young David

The context of 1 Samuel 16:7 is that of the choosing and anointing of a king over Israel. God told Samuel that this king would be one of the sons of Jesse from Bethlehem. Jesse had eight sons, some of whom were evidently very handsome, tall and robust. God's choice, however, was David. David was Jesse's youngest son, and he was not actually there when Samuel went to Jesse, for at the time he was out herding the sheep. Jesse's first, fine seven sons were paraded before Samuel. When Samuel saw Jesse's son Eliab, he said, 'Surely the LORD's anointed is before Him!' (1 Sam. 16:6). Others of Jesse's sons were also paraded, but the Bible records, 'Samuel said to Jesse, "The LORD has not chosen these."' (1 Sam. 16:10). Young David was finally sent for – fetched from the flocks outside – and, unlikely candidate though David seemed, the Bible tells us 'The LORD said, "Arise, anoint him; for this is the one!" Then Samuel took the horn of oil and anointed him in the midst of his brothers; and the Spirit of the LORD came upon David from that day forward' (1 Sam. 16:12, 13).

In the story of David, therefore, outward appearances, age and physique were deceptive. David was God's choice. God looked beyond the outward to David's inward, spiritual qualities. In spite of the flaws and faults which Scripture reveals of David, God yet said of him: 'I have found David the son of Jesse, a man after My own heart, who will do all My will' (Acts 13:22). In David, God's anointed king, we have a clear 'type' of *the* anointed one, the Lord Jesus Christ. He is 'Great David's Greater Son' (See Acts 13:22, 23), the 'KING OF KINGS AND LORD OF LORDS' (Rev. 19:16).

Our inward and outward appearance

In the Western world, the fashion, cosmetic, and hair and beauty industries are worth millions to the economy. These are all concerned with externals – the outward appearance we present to the world, our facade, our 'front'. Our verse in 1 Samuel 16:7, though, reminds us that God's view of us is more than 'skin-deep'. 'For the LORD does not see as man sees; for man looks at the outward appearance, but the LORD looks at the heart.'

In the Bible, 'the heart' refers not so much to the physical organ which pumps the blood around the body, but to the 'inner man' – the real 'you' – our very nature, our thoughts, motives and desires. The heart is the seat of the soul, the core of one's being from which all else flows. Hence Proverbs 4:23 reads, 'Keep your heart with all diligence, for out of it spring the issues of life.'

If we know our own 'hearts', the fact that 'the LORD looks at the heart' is very unsettling indeed. It is unsettling as, truth be told, we know our hearts are less than pure. That the all-seeing God looks beyond the outward appearance we present to the world and sees our innermost 'hearts' is the unanimous testimony of Scripture. 'Every way of a man is right in his own eyes, but the LORD weighs the hearts' (Prov. 21:2). 'I, the LORD, search the heart, I test the mind ...' (Jer. 17:10). 'And there is no creature hidden from His sight, but all things are naked and open to the eyes of Him to whom we must give account' (Heb. 4:13).

In medical practice, the correct diagnosis always precedes the cure. The Bible's diagnosis of us is that we have 'heart trouble'. We are wrong 'at heart' – the core of our being. 'The heart is deceitful above all things, and desperately wicked; who can know it?' (Jer. 17:9). The awareness of our malady is the first step in seeking a remedy. It is the awareness of our sinful hearts which leads us to seek salvation. We sin because we are sinners 'at heart'. We are sinners by nature. Jesus Himself taught that sinful deeds are the result of a sinful heart – the fruit grows from the root. Jesus said, 'For from within, out of the heart of men, proceed evil thoughts, adulteries, fornications, murders, thefts, covetousness, wickedness, deceit, lewdness, an evil eye, blasphemy, pride, foolishness' (Mark 7:21, 22).

A New Heart

Our greatest need, then, is for forgiveness and goodness. The good news is that God, in amazing grace, has met our deepest 'heart' need. He sent His own Son into the world to die on the cross for our sins and so procure our eternal forgiveness. He gives us the gift of His Holy Spirit within us to transform our hearts so that we desire and are enabled to live a life pleasing to God. He gave us Jesus for our eternal life. He gives us His Holy Spirit for our internal life! God's wonderful promise to us in Christ is: 'I will cleanse you … I will give you a new heart … I will put My Spirit within you and cause you to walk in My statutes, and you will keep My judgments and do them' (Ezek. 36:25-27).

Sadly, our hearts are corrupt. We have inherited Adam's sinful nature. Our greatest need is a spiritual transformation from within. God, in His grace, has provided this for us. He has met us in our need. He has done what we are incapable of doing. He sent His Son to procure our forgiveness. He sends His Spirit to live within us. All is not hopeless for the corrupt of heart! There is a God who saves. The Christian testimony is that 'He saved us, through the washing of regeneration and renewing of the Holy Spirit, whom He poured out on us abundantly through Jesus Christ our Saviour' (Titus 3:5, 6).

20

The salt of the earth

We describe someone as 'the salt of the earth' when we like them and appreciate their being around us. A faithful friend who stands by us through thick and thin may thus be described by us as 'the salt of the earth'. The writer of the Book of Proverbs tells us, 'A friend loves at all times, and a brother is born for adversity' (Prov. 17:17). An elderly, housebound person, whose carer visits her daily and attends to her needs, may also describe her carer as 'the salt of the earth'. 'Salt of the earth-type' characters tend to be the unsung heroes who are strangers to the glare of the media, yet appreciated more than any well-known celebrity. It has been well said that 'One person cannot change the world, but you can change the world for one person.'

The expression 'the salt of the earth' stems from some words of the Lord Jesus in His 'Sermon on the Mount'. Strictly, the words here apply only to Christians – disciples of Jesus in all ages; those born again by His Spirit and redeemed by His precious blood. Jesus says to them: 'You are the salt of the earth; but if the salt loses its flavour, how shall it be seasoned? It is then good for nothing but to be thrown out and trampled underfoot by men' (Matt. 5:13).

What, though, did Jesus mean when He described His followers as 'salt' and urged them to actually act as 'salt'?

The Covenant

In Leviticus 2:13 we read of 'the salt of the covenant of your God'. Salt, therefore, was a 'sign of the covenant'[1]. The 'covenant' is a

---

1. R. K. Harrison, 'Salt' in *The New Bible Dictionary,* Third Edition, Inter-Varsity Press, (Leicester, 1996), p.1046.

central theme of the Bible – a Book which is divided into the old and new covenants. The covenant refers to the unbreakable bond which God effects between Himself and His people – His commitment to their earthly and eternal welfare – and the corresponding faithfulness He expects from them in return. In the covenant, God pledges, 'I will be their God, and they shall be My people' (Jer. 31:33). When this is so, all is well and all can only be well.

> *[Salt] was often used among Oriental peoples for ratifying agreements, so that salt became the symbol of fidelity and constancy. In the levitical cereal offerings (Lev. 2:13), salt was used as a preservative to typify the eternal nature of the 'covenant of salt' existing between God and Israel.*

So, when the Lord Jesus describes His followers as 'salt', He is simply enjoining us to be who we are by grace. 'You are the salt of the earth.' He is exhorting us to be, and to live as, the covenant people of God, bound to Him by the cords of love. He is exhorting us to be faithful to Him, as He is faithful to us. He is reminding us of God's eternal commitment to us and the loving obligation which we owe Him in return, to love, honour, obey and serve Him. 'You are the salt of the earth.' It is an encouragement to rejoice in God's grace to us. It is an exhortation to live to the praise of God's grace to us.

A Preservative

In the ancient world, salt was used as a food preservative. This was vital in a warm climate, well before the invention of refrigeration. Salt was rubbed into food to prevent decay and corruption.

We need no reminder that we live in a morally decayed and corrupt world. Sin has permeated every area of society. Christians, then, in being 'salt', are called to play their part in 'stopping the rot'. Think, for instance, of the foul language that is heard in the average office – swearing, blasphemy, profanity, etc. But God may place us in such an environment. If so, we are called to act as salt there – to be pure and wholesome. This will be reflected even in the way we speak. The Christian's very speech will be different from the speech of the unregenerate. 'Let your speech always be with grace, seasoned with salt, that you may know how you ought to answer each one' (Col. 4:6).

In a morally decayed and decaying world, therefore, our Christian calling to be 'salt' is a calling to be 'blameless and harmless, children of God without fault in the midst of a crooked and perverse generation …' (Phil. 2:15).

Flavour

Salt has been used for flavouring since time immemorial. The British have a national dish. Chips! Chips without salt, though, are somewhat insipid. Christ is thus exhorting His followers to be wholesome and agreeable. May we never be 'unsavoury' but winsome, 'showing all good fidelity, that [we] may adorn the doctrine of God our Saviour in all things' (Titus 2:10). A searching question to ask ourselves is this: 'When people see me, do they desire to know more about the Christian faith, or do I just leave a bad taste in their mouth?'

Salt also makes us thirsty. Our life and witness, therefore, are also to make others thirsty – thirsty for Jesus, who gives the invitation, 'If anyone thirsts, let him come to Me and drink' (John 7:37). Jesus alone can give the water of life, for Jesus is the water of life for parched, thirsty, dying souls.

'You are the salt of the earth,' says the Lord Jesus to His disciples in all ages. In summary, it was an exhortation to live as the covenant people of God, to be a preservative, a counter-force in a corrupt world, and to be pure, wholesome and winsome, attracting people to the Christ whom we claim to know and love. All this really is achievable by God's grace and by His Spirit working within us. In exhorting us to be salt, Jesus is commanding all Christians to actually live as Christians and have a Christian effect in the society in which God has placed them. If not, we are not really fulfilling our chief end. If not, 'gentle Jesus' actually rebukes us as being 'good for nothing'.

21

'Let him that is without sin be the first to cast a stone'

'Let him who is without sin … be the first to throw a stone …' (John 8:7, ESV). This saying is another biblical saying that has permeated the English language. We use it to condemn someone who condemns someone! Someone criticizes someone for a foolish course of action at work. The reply to this might be, 'Don't be too harsh. We all make mistakes and slip up. Let him who is without sin be the first to cast a stone.'

In the temple at Jerusalem

Our saying originates from a curious incident in the life of the Lord Jesus Christ. While teaching in the temple early one morning, He was interrupted when 'the scribes and Pharisees brought to Him a woman caught in adultery' (John 8:3). 'They said to Him, "Teacher, this woman was caught in adultery, in the very act. Now Moses, in the law, commanded us that such should be stoned. But what do You say?"' (John 8:4, 5).

Adultery is a heinous sin. God commands, 'You shall not commit adultery' (Exod. 20:14). Adultery is a violation of the marriage vow to be faithful to one's spouse alone. Adultery thus wrecks a marriage and destroys the family unit which is the basic building block of society, causing society itself to crumble. In the days of the Bible, stoning was the penalty for adultery. Adulterers and adulteresses were stoned to death. Leviticus 20:10 pronounced: 'The man who commits adultery with another man's wife, he who commits adultery with his neighbour's wife, the adulterer and the adulteress shall surely be put to death.'

A Divine Dilemma

In bringing this unnamed adulteress to Jesus, the motivation of the scribes and Pharisees was not solely a zeal for the law of God. John records that they were out to trap Jesus. 'This they said, testing Him, that they might have something of which to accuse Him' (John 8:6). Humanly speaking, they had put Jesus into a dilemma for:

- If He had replied, 'Just turn a blind eye to what she has done, and let her go,' His critics could have accused Him of making light of the law of God, suggesting that adultery is not such a grave sin, and that God does not actually mean what He says.

- If He had responded 'Yes, the law of God is the law of God. Stone her at once,' His reputation as the friend and Saviour of sinners would have been lost.

A Divine Response

The Lord Jesus' response was not to condone the woman's behaviour – but He did not condemn her, either. Rather, it was as if He reminded her accusers that 'There is none righteous, no, not one' (Rom. 3:10), '[f]or there is no difference; for all have sinned and fall short of the glory of God' (Rom. 3:22, 23). Jesus welcomed the stone-throwers, but with one caveat: only sinless stone-throwers could participate. He issued the challenge to the woman's accusers: 'Let him who is without sin … be the first to throw a stone at her' (John 8:7, ESV). Her accusers' consciences were pricked. They all shuffled away guiltily. 'Then those who heard it, being convicted by their conscience, went out one by one, beginning with the oldest even to the last. And Jesus was left alone, and the woman standing in the midst' (John 8:9). The incident closes on a touching, hopeful note: 'When Jesus … saw no one but the woman, He said to her, "Woman, where are those accusers of yours? Has no one condemned you?" She said, "No one, Lord." And Jesus said to her, "Neither do I condemn you; go and sin no more"' (John 8:10, 11).

Saved by Grace

The unnamed adulteress of John 8 is, therefore, a trophy of grace. As such, every Christian can relate to her. 'Neither do I condemn you.' 'There is therefore now no condemnation to those who are in Christ Jesus' (Rom. 8:1). Knowing the pardon of Jesus, she and we begin to live a new life, and are motivated to please God – not to obtain mercy, but in response to the great mercy we have received.

The incident in John 8 does raise the question as to how God can show mercy to sinners without violating His law. And the answer to the question is found in the cross of Christ. In sending His own Son to die in the place of sinners and bear their penalty for breaking His law, God found a way both to condemn sin and pardon the believing sinner. The cross is the supreme demonstration of both the justice and mercy of God – 'that He might be just and the justifier of the one who has faith in Jesus' (Rom. 3:26).

The gospel proclaims that Christ 'Himself bore our sins in His own body on the tree' (1 Pet. 2:24). It is because of the cross that Jesus is able to say to every sinner who turns to Him, 'Neither do I condemn you; go and sin no more.'

A Little Bird Told Me

'Neither do I condemn thee!'
O words of wondrous grace,
Thy sins were borne upon the cross,
Believe and go in peace.

'Neither do I condemn thee!'
For there is therefore now
'No condemnation' for thee
As at the cross you bow.

'Neither do I condemn thee!'
I came not to condemn;
I came from God to save thee
And turn thee from thy sin.

'Neither do I condemn thee!'
O praise the God of grace!
O praise His Son, our Saviour,
For this His word of peace!

'Neither do I condemn thee!'
O sing it o'er and o'er
'Neither do I condemn thee!'
Go and sin no more.

(ATTRIBUTED TO DANIEL W. WHITTLE)

22

'It's a labour of love'

We use the description 'a labour of love' to refer to work we do with a motivation and for a reward that is other than strictly financial. For example, here is a person who gives up a well-paid job to care for his elderly parents, for he does not want them to be put into an eventide home. Here is a qualified accountant who gives of his accountancy expertise to his local church for free. Here is a former boxer who spends his evenings training youngsters how to box, hoping that this will teach them discipline, and keep them off the streets and out of trouble. When asked why they do what they do, such people might reply, 'It's all a labour of love.'

As well as being mentioned in 1 Thessalonians 1:3 and Hebrews 6:10, the thought and spirit of work being lovingly undertaken is found throughout the Bible. For instance, in Genesis 29 we read how Jacob fell in love with Rachel, the daughter of his uncle Laban. Genesis 29:18 tells us 'Now Jacob loved Rachel; so he said [to Laban], "I will serve you seven years for Rachel your younger daughter."' That is, Jacob offered Laban seven years of work in order to gain the hand of Rachel in marriage. Genesis 29:20 then tells us 'So Jacob served seven years for Rachel, and they seemed only a few days to him because of the love he had for her.' Jacob's seven years of labour then were 'a labour of love'. The reality, though, was not to be simple. Jacob, who was well known for his trickery, was then himself a victim of trickery. When the seven years were up, Laban deceived Jacob into marrying Leah, his elder daughter – possibly by a deceitful use of the veil worn by women in those days. After some negotiation, Jacob did marry Rachel – the condition being that Jacob had to work another seven years for Laban. The skulduggery apart, though, Jacob's true desire was eventually realized. Rachel became his wife. In due course, Rachel gave him two sons – Joseph and Benjamin.

Jacob's service to Laban to gain the hand of Rachel was a 'labour of love'. The seven years flew. 'Jacob served seven years for Rachel, and they seemed only a few days to him because of the love he had for her' (Gen. 29:20).

Christian labour

True Christian service is always 'a labour of love'. Those truly saved by the grace of God in Christ can only be motivated to live, please and serve Him in a life of gratitude. Salvation is all of grace. Service is all of gratitude – motivated by a love for God in response to the great love He has shown to us. His 'service' for us in Christ always precedes our service for Him. His love always takes precedence. This has always been so. In Old Testament times, we note that the Ten Commandments – the duty God requires of us – are prefaced by an affirmation of what God has already done for His people in redeeming mercy: 'I am the LORD your God, who brought you out of the land of Egypt, out of the house of bondage' (Exod. 20:2). If, in Old Testament times, service and obedience to God were a response of gratitude to His prevenient grace, how much more is it 'this side' of Calvary and the empty tomb ... 'God demonstrates His own love toward us, in that while we were still sinners, Christ died for us' (Rom. 5:8). 'In this is love, not that we loved God, but that He loved us and sent His Son to be the propitiation for our sins' (1 John 4:10).

Faith works

Our motives for serving God are a touchstone to test whether our Christian faith is the genuine Christian faith of the Bible or not. All non-Christian and sub-Christian religions generally have this in common: salvation by works. Serving God here is with a view to gaining His favour. Salvation is viewed in terms of human graft and not in terms of divine grace. Biblical Christianity, however, proclaims that salvation is by God's mercy, not by human merit. And once this transforming mercy is received, we are motivated and empowered to serve God. We serve not to gain His favour but rather because we are the recipients of His favour.

True Christians, therefore, are anxious to do God's will and to worship Him. Their motive in doing this is the motive of love – a response to the love of God in Christ at Calvary. It was Paul who proclaimed, 'For by grace you have been saved through faith, and that not of yourselves; it is the gift of God, not of works, lest anyone should boast' (Eph. 2:8, 9). And in the very next verse he went on to say, 'For we are His workmanship, created in Christ Jesus for good works, which God prepared beforehand that we should walk in them' (Eph. 2:10).

Blessed are those who know the love of God and love Him in return. 'For this is the love of God, that we keep His commandments. And His commandments are not burdensome' (1 John 5:3). Being a bond-slave of Christ is perfect liberty, for His yoke is easy and His burden is light. The service of God is nothing but 'a labour of love' for those who are the recipients of His saving grace.

> *Happy are they, they that love God,*
> *Whose hearts have Christ confessed;*
> *Who by His cross have found their life,*
> *And 'neath His yoke their rest.*

A Little Bird Told Me

Glad is the praise, sweet are the songs
When they together sing;
And strong the prayers that bow the ear,
Of heaven's eternal King.

(CHARLES COFFIN, 1676–1749)

23

He's fallen from grace

The words 'He's fallen from grace' are popularly used to describe a public figure who has been found to be acting hypocritically and, consequently, has brought disgrace on himself. His action has caused him to be out of favour with the general public.

Here, for example, is a politician known for promoting 'family values'. He has often been photographed with his wife and children. But he is then found to have had an affair with his secretary. His deeds have contradicted his words. His wife divorces him. His reputation is tarnished. He has 'fallen from grace'. Sadly, such happenings are not unknown even in Christian leadership circles.

The expression 'fallen from grace' is found in one of the earliest letters of the New Testament. In Galatians 5:4, Paul writes, 'You have become estranged from Christ, you who attempt to be justified by law; *you have fallen from grace*' (emphasis mine). Here, though, the words 'fallen from grace' are used in a way somewhat different from the way the expression is popularly used and understood today. Paul's use of the term needs a careful exposition in the light of its immediate context, as well as in the light of the whole Bible.

Once saved, always saved
The good news of the Bible is that a true Christian – one truly saved by the triune God – cannot 'fall from grace'. The Bible teaches the eternal security of the soul united to Christ in saving faith. God saves, and God preserves. Jesus said of His own sheep: 'I give them eternal life, and they shall never perish;

neither shall anyone snatch them out of My hand' (John 10:28). Christian salvation would not be the good news that it is if it were not certain – if we could be saved today and lost tomorrow. True Christian salvation, however, is sure, for the Bible teaches that Almighty God is as active in keeping His children as He was in initially saving His children. 'Now to Him who is able to keep you from stumbling, and to present you faultless before the presence of His glory with exceeding joy…' (Jude 24).

The Province of Galatia

With the above in mind, to what was Paul referring when he wrote to the Galatians, telling them, 'You have become estranged from Christ, you who attempt to be justified by law; you have fallen from grace'?

Paul was actually responding to events which had overtaken him in Galatia. When he first visited the Province, he preached the gospel of Christ crucified. Many of the Galatians gladly embraced this gospel. They were saved solely by the grace of God in the crucified Christ, and many new churches were formed. Sadly, though, when Paul left the Province, false teachers took his place. They taught that it was necessary to keep the Jewish ceremonial law to be saved. They taught that salvation was by human works – as if the grace of God in Christ was insufficient. Sadly, some of the Galatians were taken in by this false teaching. They had believed in Christ, but now they acted as though they had not. They acted as though their salvation depended on what they did, not on what Christ had done. They acted as though salvation depended on human graft instead of divine grace. They had thus fallen away from the sphere of grace. On hearing this, Paul hurriedly dictated the epistle to the Galatians. He wrote an indignant defence of the gospel of saving grace: 'You have

become estranged from Christ, you who attempt to be justified
by law; you have fallen from grace.'

> The severity of the Apostle's language is meant to disabuse
> the Galatians of their misguided enthusiasm for the law.
> For to seek justification by one's own works according to
> the law implies a severance from Christ as the provider
> of righteousness and a non-reliance upon God's grace as
> the source of salvation. 'Christ's method of justification is
> wholly of grace, and those who rely on law and merit are
> in opposition to grace – are fallen out of it. The clause
> here has really no bearing on the doctrine of the persever-
> ance of the saints, or on their possible apostasy' [a quote
> from Eadie]. Those who are saints take heed of such
> warnings and persevere in their calling; those who are not,
> often show it by publicly separating themselves from that
> domain of grace to which they never truly belonged.[1]

Grace, 'tis a charming sound

Salvation by the sheer grace of God is the distinguishing mark of
biblical Christianity and the touchstone of true religion. It is this
which separates the Christian faith from all other religions. Grace
refers to God's unmerited favour and love to the undeserving
and ill-deserving. In Christ, His grace became incarnate. Instead
of condemning us for our sins, He sent His Son to save us from
our sins and reconcile us to Himself, so that we might be able to
glorify Him and enjoy Him for ever. 'By grace you have been saved
through faith and this is not your own doing. It is the gift of God, not
because of works, lest any man should boast. (See Eph. 2:8, 9.)

When we know our own hearts and weakness, how glad we
are that salvation really is solely by God's grace, and is so from
the beginning to the end, from election to glory. It is the grace
of God that makes the Christian gospel the Good News that it

---

1. G. B. Wilson, *Galatians,* The Banner of Truth Trust, (Edinburgh,
   1973), p.101

is. Ensure then that you don't make the Galatians' mistake and believe any 'gospel' or teaching which militates against the sheer grace of God in Christ on the cross. Keep the grace of God in Christ central. Keep the main thing the main thing.

> *Grace, 'tis a charming sound,*
> *Harmonious to the ear.*
> *Heaven with the echo shall resound,*
> *And all the earth shall hear!*
>
> *'Twas grace that wrote my name*
> *In life's eternal book;*
> *'Twas grace that gave me to the Lamb,*
> *Who all my sorrows took.*
>
> *Saved by grace alone –*
> *This is all my plea;*
> *Jesus died for sinful men,*
> *And Jesus died for me!*

(PHILIP DODDRIDGE, 1702–51,

AND AUGUSTUS MONTAGUE TOPLADY, 1740–78)

24

A fly in the ointment

We use the expression 'a fly in the ointment' to refer to an unintended flaw or impairment in something which is otherwise good. We might enjoy participating in sport, for instance – but the sport we love always has the risk of injury. We plan a short holiday away – but our travel plans are disrupted. Our train is cancelled and we arrive late. Then we are smitten by a slight illness which, while not cancelling our holiday completely, nevertheless makes it less than ideal. We've been affected by 'a fly in the ointment'.

Consider, also, the various divine ordinances established for our benefit. The family is one such ordinance – yet when more than one person lives in close proximity under one roof, there is a danger of friction. Work is another divine ordinance, not to mention a practical necessity for most. Yet few people know what it is like to earn a living without experiencing stresses and strains as they do so. Everything on earth always seems to have 'a fly in the ointment'.

The term 'a fly in the ointment' has its origin in the Old Testament Book of Ecclesiastes. We read that '[d]ead flies make the perfumer's ointment give off an evil odour; so a little folly outweighs wisdom and honour' (Eccles. 10:1, RSV). The 'Preacher' is saying here that something pleasant – such as fragrant ointment – can be marred by something as small as a fly which, somewhat foolishly, flutters into the perfume and suffocates itself . He also is saying that good and honourable men can ruin their reputation by just one lapse into folly and sin. Our daily papers thrive on the latter.

The Book of Ecclesiastes was written by King Solomon, some 900 years B.C., at the end of his long and colourful life. Its twelve chapters consist of his observations on the mysteries, perplexities and apparent irrationalities of our earthly existence 'under the sun'. '"Vanity of vanities," says the Preacher; "vanity of vanities, all is vanity. What profit has a man from all his labour in which he toils under the sun?"' (Eccles. 1:2, 3). Almost everything on earth seems so absurd, frustrating, futile and nonsensical when you analyse it – muses Solomon with exasperation … The Book of Ecclesiastes can be a bit depressing to read. Solomon reinforces what we all find out by harsh experience – that life does not always make sense. But we are not to read Ecclesiastes in isolation. The book is not to be read apart from the wider reference to the revelation we have in the whole Bible. The Bible reveals that there is a God who under-stands all things, and this God loves His children with an everlast-ing love. Whatever our present difficulties and discouragements, 'it will be well with those who fear God' (Eccles. 8:12).

'A fly in the ointment …' 'Dead flies make the perfumer's ointment give off an evil odour …' (Eccles. 10:1). The Bible is reminding us here that we live in a fallen, imperfect world, and that we are not to seek our ultimate satisfaction in the fragile, temporary things of earth, but in the eternal God revealed supremely in the Lord Jesus Christ. The best things of earth have a built-in capacity and capability of failing and disappointing. But God never fails or disappoints. Being made in the image of God, it is in the God of the Bible that we find our ultimate fulfilment and satisfaction.

What is the chief end of man?
Man's chief end is to glorify God, and to enjoy Him for ever.[1]

The Bible frequently reminds and warns the Christian of the tem-porary and fragile nature of life on earth. 'The form of this world is passing away' (1 Cor. 7:31). 'For the things which are seen

---

1. *The Westminster Shorter Catechism,* Question 1

are temporary, but the things which are not seen are eternal' (2 Cor. 4:18). Hence, the Bible enjoins the Christian to 'seek those things which are above, where Christ is, sitting at the right hand of God. Set your mind on things above, not on things on the earth' (Col. 3:1, 2). Yet how often do we get overly entangled with the pleasures and responsibilities of earth – 'the cares of this world, the deceitfulness of riches, and the desires for other things …' (Mark 4:19). When we do, God in His wisdom and mercy sends us 'a fly in the ointment' – something to mar our pleasure. Such weans us off the temporal and gets us back on the eternal. Such takes our attention and affection off the 'vain' things of earth and realigns us to those 'solid joys and lasting treasure none but Zion's children know'.[2]

As this world is not our eternal home, we must expect that we will often experience 'a fly in the ointment' as we journey through it. We will experience disillusionments. Our God sends them so that we do not get unduly settled and comfortable here, and tempted to think that our stay here is for ever.

The good news is that in the flawless life that is to come for the believer, there will be no more 'flies in the ointment'. They will be both eradicated and unnecessary. There our full joy and satisfaction will be in God Himself, free from all distractions and temptations without and within. It is written of the eternal kingdom of heaven that 'God Himself will be with them and be their God. And God will wipe away every tear from their eyes; there shall be no more death, nor sorrow, nor crying. There shall be no more pain, for the former things have passed away' (Rev. 21:3, 4). For the Christian, perfection will never be enjoyed in this life, but only in the life to come.

---

2. (From John Newton's hymn, *Glorious things of thee are spoken*.)

The following hymn summarizes much of what we have considered about there being 'a fly in the ointment' here on earth – living in a world which, while often pleasurable, is also characterized by being precarious, fragile and flawed as well.

My God I thank Thee who hast made
The earth so bright;
So full of splendour and of joy,
Beauty and light!
So many glorious things are here,
Noble and right.

I thank Thee too that Thou hast made
Joy to abound;
So many gentle thoughts and deeds,
Circling us round,
That in the darkest spot of earth,
Some love is found.

I thank Thee more that all our joy
Is touched with pain;
That shadows fall on brightest hours,
That thorns remain!
So that earth's bliss may be our guide,
And not our chain.

For Thou who knowest, Lord, how soon
Our weak heart clings;
Hast given us joys, tender and true,
Yet all with wings!
So that we see, gleaming on high,
Diviner things.

I thank Thee, Lord, that Thou hast kept
The best in store:
We have enough yet not too much
To long for more!
A yearning for a deeper peace,
Not known before.

A fly in the ointment

I thank Thee, Lord, that here our souls
Though amply blest,
Can never find, although they seek,
A perfect rest!
Nor ever shall, until they lean
On Jesus' breast.

(ADELAIDE ANNE PROCTER, 1825–64)

25

'I've escaped by the skin of my teeth'

The expression 'to escape by the skin of my teeth' is used when we have avoided a catastrophe by the narrowest of margins. Someone suddenly pulls out of a side road in front of us when we are driving. We slam on our brakes and only just avoid a crash. The passenger in our car might say 'Phew! That was a near squeak. We've escaped by the skin of our teeth.'

The expression 'to escape by the skin of my teeth' has a very ancient pedigree, as it is taken from the Book of Job, which, being written in the time of the Patriarchs some 2,000 years B.C., is believed to be one of the oldest books in the world.

In the providential will and purpose of God, Job experienced severe suffering. In a very short time he lost his wealth, children and health. Bemoaning his severe plight and God's mysterious dealings with him, he said in exasperation: 'My bone clings to my skin and to my flesh, and *I have escaped by the skin of my teeth*' (Job 19:20, emphasis mine). It is debated as to just what Job really meant here. Our teeth are not actually covered with skin, but enamel. The skin on Job's body was badly affected by boils and sores when he spoke these words. Perhaps Job had lost his teeth and only had his gums left … Job was suffering physical and mental agony. He felt as though he had been skinned alive. He felt that the only skin he had left was the skin on his teeth which he actually did not have! Job was thus obviously speaking metaphorically. Perhaps he was saying that while he was still alive, his health, feelings and situation were such that he was as good as dead.

Today, we take the expression 'to escape by the skin of my teeth' to refer to the avoidance of trouble, calamity or even death by a very fine hair's breadth. We are left relieved that what almost happened did not actually happen. The experience behind the phrase has an application both to the non-Christian and to the Christian.

The Non-Christian

Near-death experiences, if sanctified by God, are His wake-up calls. They remind us that this world is very uncertain. We can never say for certain that we will live to see tomorrow. The shocks of life – illness, the death of a loved one, the loss of a job or our health – wake us up and remind us that this world is extremely fragile. There is eternity to be reckoned with. Eternity is near. There is a heaven to be gained, a hell to be shunned, a God to face and, thankfully, a Saviour who saves. 'Prepare to meet your God' (Amos 4:12). It was C. S. Lewis who stated that pain is God's megaphone to rouse a deaf world. When all is smooth and plain-sailing, we can get too comfortable and complacent. The Bible, though, warns us that 'it is appointed for men to die once, but after this the judgment' (Heb. 9:27). How do we prepare for eternity? How can we be confident when we face God? The Bible's answer is 'through the Lord Jesus Christ'. In His death alone, we find pardon for sin. His righteousness alone – imputed to us, received by faith – is that which gives us confidence in the day of judgment and final reckoning. The Bible says, 'Therefore, having been justified by faith, we have peace with God through our Lord Jesus Christ' (Rom. 5:1) and, 'Having now been justified by His blood, we shall be saved from wrath through Him' (Rom. 5:9).

'I've escaped by the skin of my teeth'

Look, Father, look on His anointed Face,
And only look on us as found in Him.
Look not on our misusings of Thy grace,
Our prayer so languid and our faith so dim;
For lo! between our sins and their reward,
We set the Passion of Thy Son our Lord.

(WILLIAM BRIGHT, 1824–1901)

The Christian

'I have escaped by the skin of my teeth.' Eternity is near – yet it is so easy to get a wrong perspective, and become unduly entangled with the temporal matters of time and earth. In His mercy, God gives us reminders that this world is not eternal. He sends disappointments. Disappointments are 'His appointments'. We are to hold lightly to the passing things of time. If we grip them too tightly with our hands, God will see that they are prised away from us. He only has our eternal welfare at heart. He would have us know and enjoy the true and lasting riches – 'the unsearchable riches of Christ' (Eph. 3:8) – rather than the passing, peripheral and frivolous 'toys' of this world. Paul thus gave the exhortation to all Christians: 'If then you were raised with Christ, seek those things which are above, where Christ is, sitting at the right hand of God. Set your mind on things above, not on things on the earth. For you died, and your life is hidden with Christ in God. When Christ who is our life appears, then you also will appear with Him in glory' (Col. 3:1-4).

'I have escaped by the skin of my teeth.' Our reaction when we experience such 'escapes' reveals much about our spiritual condition. Do we carry on unaffected? Or do we turn to God in greater repentance, faith and grateful thanksgiving?

When he uttered the expression we have considered, Job was in the dark depths. But just a few verses later he rose to the heights of faith, and affirmed that, his present suffering notwithstanding: 'I know that my Redeemer lives, and He shall stand at last on the earth; and after my skin is destroyed, this I know, that in my flesh I shall see God' (Job 19:25, 26).

It is this personal knowledge of the Redeemer that makes an infinity of difference to life, suffering and eternity.

26

'He's a good Samaritan'

A 'good Samaritan' is one who helps us when we are in difficulty, need or distress. The Samaritans is an organization which provides a 24-hour 'listening ear' telephone service for those who have reached the end of their tether, and who need a sympathetic ear to talk to. The Samaritans, we are told, have prevented many suicides over the years.

In Luke 10:30-37, the Lord Jesus tells the 'Parable of the Good Samaritan'. It is one of His most well-known parables. A lawyer asked the Lord Jesus, 'Teacher, what shall I do to inherit eternal life?' (Luke 10:25), that is, what must he do to know the life and joy of God now and for ever? In reply, Jesus directed the lawyer to the law of God. The law of God may be summarized in two commandments: (a) Love the Lord God sincerely and wholeheartedly and (b) Love your neighbour as you love yourself. Of course, the Lord Jesus knew well that no one on earth – Himself excepted – has ever fulfilled these two commandments. The law does not save us, but rather shows us that we need to be saved. The lawyer though – in the usual debating style of the day – asked Jesus to define and expand His terms. He asked that the second commandment be clarified. He asked, 'And who is my neighbour?' (Luke 10:29). In response, the Lord Jesus told 'The Parable of the Good Samaritan'. The parable, rather than answering the question 'Who is my neighbour?', actually poses a more pertinent question. It poses the practical question: 'To whom can I be a neighbour?'

On the Jericho road

The road from Jerusalem to Jericho drops some 3,300 feet in seventeen miles. It is a desolate, rocky territory, well-known in Jesus' day for its bandits. The 'Parable of the Good Samaritan', in which a man was brutally mugged on this road, may well have been taken from an actual incident. Having been robbed and assaulted, the man lay half-dead at the side of the road. A priest and a Levite saw him lying there, but they passed by hurriedly on the other side. We can only speculate as to why. The hero of the parable, though, was an unlikely one. Sectarianism is not new. In Jesus' day, there was both racial and religious hostility between the Jews and the Samaritans, but it was one of the despised Samaritans who halted on his journey upon seeing the half-dead man lying there. He stopped and had compassion on him. He cleaned and bound up his wounds and took him to an inn for recovery and recuperation, all at his own expense. Considering the long-standing animosity that existed between the Jews and the Samaritans, this was humanly inexplicable and startling. It was a Samaritan – not the religious leaders – who demonstrated something of the love, mercy and grace of God to the stricken man. The parable then ends with a practical application and exhortation, with Jesus saying: '"So which of these three do you think was neighbour to him who fell among the thieves?" And [the lawyer] said, "He who showed mercy on him." Then Jesus said to him, "Go and do likewise"' (Luke 10:36, 37).

The Good Samaritan

The original 'Good Samaritan', then, was a man who proved to be a real 'neighbour'. He gave help and relief just when and where it was needed, irrespective of the religious and racial barriers and prejudices of the day. He even gave help to one who, just a day earlier, may have spoken of him and his kin in disparaging tones. Such is the grace of God. Such is the love of Jesus. 'While we were still sinners, Christ died for us' (Rom. 5:8).

In urging all His followers to be 'Good Samaritans', Jesus is urging us to be His own ambassadors in the world – to be channels of the love and mercy we have received from Him. It is a historical fact that the compassion shown by the Good Samaritan has, ever since the parable was told, inspired and motivated countless sacrificial ministries of compassion the world over. It is the love of Christ that has built hospitals and founded schools. Countless charitable organizations are Christian in their origin. It is the love of Christ that sees a missionary leaving the comfort and familiarity of home to live in an alien culture, learn a new language and new ways in order to be able to tell others about the Saviour of sinners – One who left heaven for earth, so that we might go at last to heaven, saved by His precious blood.

Jesus Himself was the ultimate 'Good Samaritan'. Although 'He is despised and rejected by men' (Isa. 53:3), He went all the way to Calvary to procure our salvation. And Jesus would have all His followers to be Good Samaritans too – to show love and mercy to our neighbours, whoever or wherever they may be. Of course, one person cannot change the world. But you can change the world for one person – doing what you can, with what you have, where you are, for the blessing of souls and the glory of God. The Parable of the Good Samaritan is a searching one. 'Who is my neighbour?' asked the lawyer. He was being theoretical. Jesus' parable posed the practical: 'To whom can I be a neighbour?'

27

A lamb to the slaughter

The expression 'It will be like a lamb to the slaughter' was once quoted by a well-known boxer. It would be fair to say that he probably did not know he was quoting from the Bible. In order to 'hype' an impending match he was about to have for the British lightweight title, boost ticket sales and rile his opponent, he announced at a press conference preceding the match that he was sure to win easily. It would verge on a mismatch, he stated. His opponent would be 'like a lamb led to the slaughter'. The expression is commonly used to refer to a one-sided, unequal contest.

Isaiah's Prophecy

The expression 'a lamb led to the slaughter' was originally a prophetic reference to the Lord Jesus Christ and His death at Calvary. The expression is found in Isaiah 53:7: 'He was oppressed and He was afflicted, yet He opened not his mouth; *He was led as a lamb to the slaughter,* and as a sheep before its shearers is silent, so He opened not his mouth.'

Some 700 years before Christ, God gave Isaiah the prophet the most remarkable view and insight into the Saviour who was to come and His atoning death at Calvary. The prophecy is in Isaiah's fifty-third chapter – a chapter inexplicable apart from the divine inspiration of the Bible. All those centuries before Christ, Isaiah was given a vision of Jesus and His death at Calvary, and an explanation of the true meaning of that death. At the heart of Isaiah's message is the gospel of Christ's substitutionary, sacrificial and saving crucifixion. Christ was to die in the place of sinners so that sinners might be saved. Writing in the prophetic past tense, the Holy Spirit guided Isaiah's pen to inscribe:

> *But He was wounded for our transgressions, He was bruised for our iniquities; the chastisement for our peace was upon Him, and by His stripes we are healed. All we like sheep have gone astray; we have turned, every one, to his own way; and the Lord has laid on Him the iniquity of us all.* (Isa. 53:5, 6)

Behold the Lamb

Isaiah's remarkable prophecy also foretold that the Christ to come would be 'led as a lamb to the slaughter'. The theme of 'the lamb' may be traced right through the Bible. A central event in Old Testament history is the Exodus – the deliverance of the people of Israel from slavery in Egypt – and central to this central event was the slaying of a lamb. The story goes as follows:

The people of Israel were in bondage in Egypt. God pronounced His judgment on the whole land. His angel of death was going to slay every firstborn of human and animal there. But God provided a way of escape from this judgment. If an unblemished lamb was taken, killed, and its blood applied to the doorpost and lintel of the home, He would accept the death of the lamb in the place of the firstborn of that house. Judgment could thus be avoided by the slaughtering of a lamb and the application of its blood. God promised, 'Now the blood shall be a sign for you on the houses where you are. And when I see the blood, I will pass over you; and the plague shall not be on you to destroy you when I strike the land of Egypt' (Exod. 12:13).

And it all happened just as God had foretold. The angel of death passed over Egypt in fearful judgment. The firstborn of Egypt were slain, and a great cry went up from their houses.

But the firstborn of Israel were spared. They were saved by the blood of the Passover lamb. A lamb had been slaughtered. Its blood had been applied. All those sheltering under that blood were saved and safe.

The Passover lamb of the Old Testament is one of the clearest types of the Christ of the New Testament. Jesus was 'led as a lamb to the slaughter'. The Christian gospel proclaims that His death and blood-shedding is the only means by which a sinner can escape the condemnation of God due to us for our sins. Christ is the true, unblemished Lamb that saves. It is the unanimous testimony of the Bible:

'For indeed Christ, our Passover, was sacrificed for us' (1 Cor. 5:7).

'In Him we have redemption through His blood, the forgiveness of sins, according to the riches of His grace' (Eph. 1:7).

' … redeemed … with the precious blood of Christ, as of a lamb without blemish and without spot' (1 Pet. 1:18, 19).

'Worthy is the Lamb who was slain' (Rev. 5:12).

The Silence of the Lamb

Isaiah's prophecy, interestingly, contains a reference to the silence of the slain lamb – 'He was oppressed and He was afflicted, yet He opened not His mouth; He was led as a lamb to the slaughter, and as a sheep before its shearers is silent, so He opened not His mouth' (Isa. 53:7). This detail was also fulfilled to the letter, as the New Testament reveals that Jesus was silent before His accusers with a silence that condemned Him to death. Before the high priest, 'Jesus kept silent' (Matt. 26:63); before

Pilate, 'He answered him not one word, so that the governor marvelled greatly' (Matt. 27:14). How, then, do we explain this silence which condemned Christ to death? The 'silence of the lamb', that is, the silence of Christ, can only be explained by considering the silence of Christ's submission and the silence of Christ's imputed guilt.

The silence of Christ's submission
God had His eternal plan of salvation to save a people for Himself and His glory. Central to this plan was the sacrifice of His Son. Christ submitted to this plan and 'became obedient to the point of death, even the death of the cross' (Phil. 2:8). The Bible reveals both the active and the passive obedience of Christ. He actively obeyed God's law. Then, on behalf of others, He passively suffered the consequences of that broken law, paying their penalty for their breaking of it – 'wounded for *our* transgressions … bruised for *our* iniquities …' (Isa. 53:5).

The silence of Christ's imputed guilt
Sadly, we all know of a very uncomfortable phenomenon described as a 'guilty silence'. Before God we are guilty. We have broken His law. We are condemned by His law. 'For by the law is the knowledge of sin' (Rom. 3:20). 'That every mouth may be stopped, and all the world may become guilty before God' (Rom. 3:19). The sinless Christ took upon Himself our guilt. He was accounted guilty so that, by believing in Him, we might be accounted righteous. Calvary's work involved a saving transaction. The sinless Christ was accounted sinful by God so that sinners who believe in Him may be acquitted. He is 'the Lamb of God who takes away the sin of the world' (John 1:29). In one of the most profound statements of the Bible, we read that 'He made

Him who knew no sin to be sin for us, that we might become the righteousness of God in Him' (2 Cor. 5:21).

So in the fullness of time, Christ, in fulfilment of prophecy, was 'led as a lamb to the slaughter.' He was led there so that sinners might be saved. The focus of the Bible is not so much on Christ's life but His death – His saving, substitutionary sacrifice for the sinner's eternal redemption.

> *Guilty, vile and helpless we;*
> *Spotless Lamb of God was He;*
> *Full atonement! Can it be?*
> *Hallelujah! What a Saviour!*

(PHILIP P. BLISS, 1838–76)

28

Manna from heaven

'Manna from heaven' popularly refers to a welcome gift or provision which someone gives us. The gift both brings us pleasure and meets a need. The provision comes just at the right time! Someone collapses in the street – but a doctor 'happens' to be passing. Someone else 'happens' to have a mobile phone. We are going through a hard time financially, and an uncle 'happens' to send us a cheque in the post. We are troubled about something, and a friend unexpectedly phones us just at that moment. A problem shared seems to be a problem halved. We receive a Christmas present perfectly in line with our interests and most helpful to our pursuing a certain hobby … all these seem 'heaven-sent'. They are like 'manna from heaven'.

In the wilderness

The original 'manna from heaven' refers to some agreeable food which God Himself sent to provide for and sustain His people. Moses states, 'The house of Israel called its name Manna. And it was like white coriander seed, and the taste of it was like wafers made with honey' (Exod. 16:31).

After the people of Israel had been delivered from slavery in Egypt, they found themselves living in the wilderness – the desert. The desert is a dry, barren place. Nothing grows there. How, then, did they survive? They did so through the gracious provision of God. He sent them bread from heaven. 'He … rained down manna on them to eat, and [gave] them of the bread of heaven. Men ate angels' food; He sent them food to the full' (Ps. 78:24, 25). The Bible records that 'the children of Israel ate manna forty years, until they came to an inhabited land; they ate manna until they came to the border of the land of Canaan' (Exod. 16:35). When they left the desert and entered the Promised Land, however, we read that 'the manna ceased on the day after they had eaten the produce of the land; and the children of Israel no longer had manna, but they ate the food of the land of Canaan that year' (Josh. 5:12). A miraculous provision of food was necessary in the dead, barren wilderness. The Promised Land, however, was not a barren land. It was a fertile land 'flowing with milk and honey' (Exod. 3:17). God's provision for His people here, therefore, was not a supernatural one but a natural one. Food was provided through the cultivation of the land. But what do we learn from the 'manna from heaven'?

Our dependence on God

The manna from heaven reminds us of our total dependence upon God. He both gives us life and He provides us with what we need to sustain our lives. It is 'in Him we live and move and have our being' (Acts 17:28). Jesus taught us to pray to God 'Give us this day our daily bread' (Matt. 6:11), that is, to trust God to provide for us one day at a time. Interestingly, the original manna was a daily provision. When more than one day's supply was hoarded faithlessly 'it bred worms and stank' (Exod. 16:20). But so that the people could keep the Sabbath without working, God provided a double portion of manna for them on the day before the Sabbath. On this day, 'it did not stink, and there were no worms in it' (Exod. 16:24, ESV).

The original manna was God's gracious provision for His peoples' sustenance. The principle still applies today. Ultimately it is God Himself who provides for all our needs – what we need to live and serve Him. 'And my God shall supply all your need according to His riches in glory by Christ Jesus' (Phil. 4:19). 'I have been young, and now am old; yet I have not seen the righteous forsaken, nor his descendants begging bread' (Ps. 37:25). God provided through supernatural means in the wilderness and through natural means in Canaan. The norm today is for God to provide for us through 'means'. He does not send us 'bread from heaven' directly, but rather provides us with work and the ability to work, so that we are able to buy our bread and provide for our families. Our dependence upon God and on His generosity is not to be used as an excuse for indolence!

Jesus: The True and Living Bread

In the light of the New Testament, we know that the manna from heaven is a picture of the Lord Jesus Christ. He is the true bread from heaven. We are composed of souls as well as bodies. What bread is to our bodies, Jesus is to our souls. He alone can satisfy the spiritual hunger of one made in the image of God, dissatisfied and restless, seeking inner satisfaction, satiation and rest. No sooner had Jesus miraculously fed over five thousand people with just five loaves and two fish, than he declared: 'I am the bread of life. He who comes to Me shall never hunger, and he who believes in Me shall never thirst' (John 6:35).

The original manna was sent by God from heaven. So was Jesus. The original manna sustained the people temporarily. Jesus saves, sustains and satisfies us eternally. Through His death on the cross – His giving up of His sinless life as an eternal sacrifice – all who believe in Him have eternal life, eternal salvation and eternal satisfaction. Jesus Himself was aware of this contrast, for He taught, 'I am the bread of life. Your fathers ate the manna in the wilderness, and are dead. This is the bread which comes down from heaven, that one may eat of it and not die. I am the living bread which came down from heaven. If anyone eats of this bread, he will live forever; and the bread that I shall give is My flesh, which I shall give for the life of the world' (John 6:48-51).

Bread only benefits us if it is taken and eaten. Salvation also is only experienced and enjoyed if Jesus is 'eaten', that is, believed in. It is by faith that we partake of the Lord Jesus Christ and His blessings and benefits.

And so we see that the God of the Bible is a God who provides. He gives 'manna from heaven'. He provides for His people's physical needs, and He has given us His Son to meet our deepest, eternal, spiritual need.

> *Thou art the Bread of life,*
> *O Lord, to me;*
> *Thy holy Word the truth*
> *That saveth me;*
> *Give me to eat and live*
> *With Thee above;*
> *Teach me to love Thy truth,*
> *For Thou art love.*

(MARY LATHBURY, 1841–1913)

29

The strait and narrow

Staying on 'the strait and narrow' popularly refers to living a good and honest life, keeping yourself out of trouble and staying on the right side of the law. Years back, there was a popular British TV comedy called *Porridge.* This was set in one of H.M. Prisons, and its chief character was one of its inmates – a wily, lovable rogue by the name of Fletcher. The series was followed up by a sequel entitled *Going Straight.* This was concerned with what happened to Fletcher once he had served his time inside.

The expression 'on the strait and narrow' originates from an exhortation and warning which the Lord Jesus gave in His famous Sermon on the Mount. There, Jesus said: 'Enter ye in at the strait gate: for wide is the gate, and broad is the way, that leadeth to destruction, and many there be which go in thereat: Because *strait* is the gate, and *narrow* is the way, which leadeth unto life, and few there be that find it' (Matt. 7:13, 14, KJV, emphasis mine).

The Twos

Did you notice the 'twos' in the Saviour's words here? There are, he said, two gates, opening on to two roads – a narrow road and a wide road. And these two roads lead to two different destinations, heaven and hell. There are also two crowds walking on these two roads. The majority crowd is on the broad road leading to hell. Only a minority enter through the narrow gate, and travel the narrow road which leads to heaven.

The Bible in general and the Lord Jesus in particular divide humanity into two stark categories – the saved and the lost. The 'black-and-white' nature of this does not sit easily with the 'inclusivity' and 'diversity' propagated by the secular world today. The secular world seeks to tolerate anyone and everything, and emphasizes shades of grey rather than stark, 'black and white' categories. Strangely, though, it will not tolerate the absolute truth of the Christian faith. The question is: Do we believe God's Word, or do we follow the prevailing ethos and popular thinking of the present? To ask the question is to answer it. Jesus pre-empted the popular thinking of today when He told of the 'way that leadeth to destruction … many there be which go in thereat'. The popular majority is not always right. People en masse can be deluded. In Proverbs 14:12, we read that 'There is a way that seems right to a man, but its end is the way of death.'

A matter of eternal life and death

If we would know eternal life, therefore, how vital it is that we get on (and stay on) 'the strait and narrow': that we enter by the narrow gate and walk the narrow way – albeit with the minority – which leads to 'life', that is, the nearer presence of God who is the source of all life, love, light and joy. The big question, therefore, is: To what was the Saviour referring when He exhorts us to 'walk the strait and narrow way'?

In the light of the whole Bible, we know that the 'strait and narrow way' which leads to eternal life is the Lord Jesus Christ Himself. He is the way. He is an exclusive Saviour. He proclaimed, 'I am the door. If anyone enters by Me, he will be saved' (John 10:9). Jesus affirmed of Himself: 'I am the way, the truth, and the life. No one comes to the Father except through Me' (John 14:6).

The Lord Jesus is the only Saviour. Eternal life is found in Him alone. It is this exclusivity of the Lord Jesus which goes completely against the grain of today's thinking, certainly in the West.

The current-day stress is on 'inclusivity' and 'diversity'. But the Bible is categorical and clear: 'Nor is there salvation in any other, for there is no other name under heaven given among men by which we must be saved' (Acts 4:12). 'And this is the testimony: that God has given us eternal life, and this life is in His Son. He who has the Son has life; he who does not have the Son of God does not have life' (1 John 5:11, 12).

'Walking the strait and narrow', then, in its biblical sense, refers to trusting the Lord Jesus and His atoning death for our eternal salvation. This might not make us popular in an age which proclaims many and varied ways of salvation – if it is concerned with salvation at all. In the light of eternity, however, how glad we will be that we believed in Jesus, and how eternally grateful we will be to the grace of God and the God of grace who chose us, sent His Son to redeem us and drew us to the foot of the cross and bestowed on us saving faith in the crucified One.

'The strait and narrow' – it is a reference to Jesus Himself. According to the Bible, He is the one and only Saviour.

> *Thou art the Way, to Thee alone,*
> *From sin and death we flee;*
> *And he who would the Father seek,*
> *Must seek Him, Lord, by Thee.*
>
> *Thou art the Way, the Truth, the Life;*
> *Grant us that Way to know,*
> *That Truth to keep, that Life to win,*
> *Whose joys eternal flow!*

> (GEORGE W. DOANE, 1799–1859)

30

'A little bird told me'

Those of us who have worked in offices that employ a number of people are aware that the working environment can sometimes resemble an unpleasant goldfish bowl. It is, perhaps, inevitable that friction will occur when people from different backgrounds work in close proximity. One of the perils of an office is 'office gossip'. We hear rumours – often salacious rumours – about our colleagues that should really be kept secret. When we ask the person spreading the rumour, 'How did you find that out about X?', the reply can sometimes be, 'A little bird told me.' The person relating the gossip does not wish to disclose the source. The gossip, though, spreads and a person's character is darkened.

The expression 'a little bird told me' originates from Ecclesiastes 10:20, where we read the admonition: 'Do not curse the king, even in your thought; do not curse the rich, even in your bedroom; *for a bird of the air may carry your voice, and a bird in flight may tell the matter*' (emphasis mine). The admonition here is telling us: 'Control your tongue.' 'Be careful how you speak. Be especially careful about how you speak about other people.' 'Little birds' chirp, of course, but cannot articulate our language. The principle behind the expression is the warning that if we say something about someone, there is always the possibility that what we have said may get back to the person concerned, causing us embarrassment and stirring up trouble. When we speak about someone to someone else, we might be overheard. The person to whom we speak may betray our confidence. The person to whom we speak may lack discretion. We should thus only say something about a person who is absent if we have the courage to say the same thing to his or her face.

The Westminster Shorter Catechism states 'The Scriptures principally teach what man is to believe concerning God, and what duty God requires of man',[1] that is, the Bible is concerned with what we are to believe to be saved, and how we are to behave once saved. Christian behaviour should permeate every facet of our lives and character – even the thoughts we think when lying in bed. A major facet of our character is our speech – how we employ our tongues. God expects Christians to employ their tongues in a Christian way, using it to extol Him and edify others, rather than blaspheme Him and cause misery to others.

Christians, therefore, should never be 'a little bird' – that is, they should never gossip about others. Gossip has marred many a happy Christian fellowship. It is also unfitting for a Christian to give ammunition to the 'little birds' around us who would be keen to take up what we say about someone and use it negatively.

The Bible has much to say about the human tongue – that small member which has a capacity for good or destruction out of all proportion to its size. Read and weigh carefully the following Scriptures:

'In the multitude of words sin is not lacking, but he who restrains his lips is wise' (Prov. 10:19).

'A talebearer reveals secrets, but he who is of a faithful spirit conceals a matter' (Prov. 11:13).

'He who guards his mouth preserves his life, but he who opens wide his lips shall have destruction' (Prov. 13:3).

1. *The Westminster Shorter Catechism,* Question 3

'A little bird told me'

'Death and life are in the power of the tongue ...' (Prov. 18:21).

'If anyone among you thinks he is religious, and does not bridle his tongue but deceives his own heart, this one's religion is useless' (James 1:26).

We are all sensitive to a greater or lesser degree. None of us would like to think that we are being talked about in a derogatory manner when we are not present. It is incumbent upon Christians, therefore, not to be party to such a practice, as our Saviour exhorts us: 'And just as you want men to do to you, you also do to them likewise' (Luke 6:31).

'A little bird told me ...' Private words can easily become public words, 'for a bird of the air may carry your voice, and a bird in flight may tell the matter' (Eccles. 10:20). The expression is a reminder to guard our tongues and not to feed the birds! We do not want to eat our words. It has been well said:

> *A careless word may kindle strife*
> *A cruel word may wreck a life*
> *A bitter word may hate instil*
> *A brutal word may smite and kill*
> *A gracious word may smooth the way*
> *A joyous word may light the day*
> *A timely word may lessen stress*
> *A loving word may heal and bless*

(ANON.)

31
Safe and sound

When we arrive back home from a long journey away, a friend might telephone us and say, 'Welcome home. I'm glad that you are back safe and sound.' If we should travel through inclement weather which disrupts our travel plans – as we sometimes do in the U.K. at Christmas-time – our friends and family at our destination might also say to us: 'We were worried you wouldn't get here! It's good to see you safe and sound.' The expression is also used in relation to building work. Builders have to be qualified. So do plumbers and electricians. It would not be wise to employ a rogue electrician. We like to feel 'safe and sound' within our homes … The modern expression for this in the workplace is 'Health and Safety'.

The Original Prodigal

The expression 'safe and sound' originates in a famous parable the Lord Jesus once told. It is known as The Parable of the Prodigal Son although it could equally be entitled The Parable of a Loving Father. The parable is recorded in Luke 15, and is the third of three parables concerning three lost 'possessions' – the parable of the lost sheep, the parable of the lost silver and the parable of the lost son.

The three parables of Luke 15 were triggered by a truism murmured resentfully by the scribes and Pharisees at Jesus that 'This man receives sinners and eats with them' (Luke 15:2). All three parables illustrate facets of divine salvation, and the consequent joy which salvation brings. Jesus said, 'I say to you, there is joy in the presence of the angels of God over one sinner who repents' (Luke 15:10).

135

The Parable of the Prodigal Son is so vivid, there is a distinct possibility that it is based on a real-life happening. In it, one of two brothers more or less told his father that he wished he, his father, were dead. He asked for the inheritance he would have in the future when his father died, took it, and went far away from home where he squandered his inheritance in the illicit thrills of 'the world, the flesh and the devil'. By doing so, he brought great disgrace on the family name. This apart, it was a joyous riot while his money lasted. But then his money ran out, poverty struck and reality bit. He had no option but to 'eat humble pie' and be a labourer to a pig farmer – very humbling indeed for a Jewish boy. Amidst the pigswill, though, he reasoned to himself: 'I'd rather be a slave of my father than a slave here. I'd be better off at home. I'm going to return home.' So off the prodigal went, back home.

But how would the young man's father treat him when he arrived home? Would he cast him out as a 'good-for-nothing'? Perhaps he should have … But no. When he arrived home, the father received him with the most joyful of welcomes and treated him not as a slave but a prince! 'When he was still a great way off, his father saw him and had compassion, and ran and fell on his neck and kissed him' (Luke 15:20).

Does God the Father really receive repentant sinners who have rebelled against Him? According to this parable, and on the authority of the Lord Jesus, we can affirm that He does. The father's grace abounded to his son. Yes, the son was undeserving and ill-deserving, but instead of ordering punishment, the father ordered the best robe to be put on him, along with a ring on his finger – a pledge of his love – and a great celebratory party to be arranged. 'For this my son was dead and is alive again; he was lost and is found' (Luke 15:24).

The other son – the prodigal's brother – had never left the family home. In the parable, he comes over as somewhat like a Pharisee. Coming back from his work, he enquired as to the partying and general commotion – 'music and dancing' (Luke 15:25). The answer he received takes us to our expression. One of his father's servants explained to him: 'Your brother has come, and because he has received him *safe and sound,* your father has killed the fatted calf' (Luke 15:27, emphasis mine).

Salvation

The Parable of the Prodigal Son is illustrative of many sides of the multi-faceted diamond which is salvation. We note, first of all, that the renegade son in the far country had a change of mind which led to a change of action. This is known in the Bible as 'repentance'. We are not saved by repentance, yet paradoxically there is no salvation without repentance:

> *Repentance unto life is a saving grace whereby a sinner, out of a true sense of his sin and apprehension of the mercy of God in Christ, doth with grief and hatred of his sin turn from it unto God, with full purpose of and endeavour after new obedience.[1]*

Secondly, we note that the Parable of the Prodigal Son – as we have intimated – shows that God the Father receives sinners when they come to Him through Christ. He actually takes them into His family, and treats them not as slaves but as His sons. 'Adoption' is the technical term for this. In the Bible, adoption is one of many synonyms for salvation:

---

1. *The Westminster Shorter Catechism,* Question 87

Adoption is an act of God's free grace whereby we are received into the number, and have a right to all the privileges of the sons of God.[2]

Finally, we note that the lost son, when back in the father's house, under his father's loving care, was now *safe and sound.* Salvation is a matter of being made 'safe and sound'. If our faith is in the crucified Saviour, we are eternally saved and eternally safe – saved from the wrath of God, eternally pardoned and adopted into God's family, never to be cast out.

Jesus is a Saviour who really saves. He saves for time and eternity. If we belong to Him, the Bible says, nothing at all 'shall be able to separate us from the love of God which is in Christ Jesus our Lord' (Rom. 8:39).

'Safe and Sound'. By the grace of God in Christ, Christians really are.

---

2. *The Westminster Shorter Catechism,* Question 34

32

Rise and shine!

I was spared the traumas of military life, as compulsory National Service ceased before I was born. My father and uncles, however, all have their tales about life in an army barracks. One such was the dubious delight of being woken up at 5.30 a.m. by a sergeant major for 'square-bashing'. The comfort of bed was, I am told, abruptly halted by his banging a dustbin lid and shouting, 'Rise and shine!' at the top of his voice. The expression means something like 'Get up and go.'

Few might realize that the expression 'Rise and shine!' is a biblical one, but it is. Isaiah 60 is a glorious prophecy concerning the Messianic age, and the prophecy begins: 'Arise, shine; for your light has come! And the glory of the LORD is risen upon you' (Isa. 60:1). The vision is breathtaking, and we have it on New Testament authority that it was fulfilled in Jesus and will yet be fulfilled in Jesus. It was fulfilled in Jesus' first coming when 'the true Light which gives light to every man' (John 1:9) came into the world; and it will yet be fulfilled in Jesus' second coming, when He will usher in God's eternal kingdom of eternal day.

The coming of the Light

' … your light has come!' … Isaiah's prophecy was fulfilled in Christ. Jesus made the stupendous claim, 'I am the light of the world. He who follows Me shall not walk in darkness, but have the light of life' (John 8:12). 'Light' in the Bible is used to signify God, truth, goodness, moral excellence, joy, safety and life. Whereas darkness is just the opposite, connoting evil, falsehood, sin, sorrow, the devil and death. As 'the light of the world', Jesus was claiming to be God, for 'God is light and in Him is no darkness at all' (1 John 1:5). As 'the light of the world', the Lord Jesus is both the unsurpassed and unsurpassable revelation of the one true God, and brings the unsurpassed and unsurpassable salvation of the one true God. John explained, 'No one has seen God at any time. The only begotten Son, who is in the bosom of the Father, He has declared Him' [that is, 'made Him known'] (John 1:18). Jesus once even said, 'He who has seen Me has seen the Father' (John 14:9). Paradoxically, Jesus, 'the light of the world', suffered the darkness of Calvary to bring us the light of God's salvation. He died to give us life. He was separated from God to reconcile us to God. He endured earthly darkness that we might bask in eternal light. Truly, then, the light of the world is Jesus. The revelation of the one true God and the salvation of the one true God is found in Him alone. 'Arise, shine; for your light has come!'

> *The whole world was lost in the darkness of sin,*
> *The Light of the world is Jesus!*
> *Like sunshine at noonday His glory shone in,*
> *The Light of the world is Jesus!*

(PHILIPP P BLISS, 1838–76)

Receiving the Light

In Ephesians 5:14, we have a distinct echo of Isaiah 60:1 – 'Arise, shine …' – in what is believed to be an early Christian hymn, sung as a new convert emerged from the waters of baptism. Ephesians 5:14 reads, 'Awake, you who sleep, arise from the dead, and Christ will give you light.'

The Bible describes Christians as being 'children of light'. In Ephesians 5:8, Paul explained to the Ephesian converts, 'For you were once darkness, but now you are light in the Lord. Walk as children of light!' Individual Christian salvation is a case of 'the glory of the Lord … risen upon you' (Isa. 60:1). Sin is a dark state as well as a damnable one. By nature, we are in the dark. We are spiritually ignorant of our lost plight and spiritual peril, and ignorant of God's remedy in Christ. The Holy Spirit of God, however, reveals this to us, and enables us to come to Jesus, the Light of the world. According to Paul, both creation and redemption are inexplicable apart from a direct and powerful act of God. 'For it is the God who commanded light to shine out of darkness who has shone in our hearts to give the light of the knowledge of the glory of God in the face of Jesus Christ' (2 Cor. 4:6). Christians are united in their testimony that 'He has delivered us from the power of darkness and conveyed us into the kingdom of the Son of His love' (Col. 1:13).

Reflecting the Light

Rise and shine! 'Arise, shine …' The exhortation is applicable to all Christians. Jesus said, 'You are the light of the world. A city that is set on a hill cannot be hidden. Nor do they light a lamp and put it under a basket, but on a lampstand, and it gives light to all who are in the house' (Matt. 5:14, 15). Having received the Light, Christians are exhorted to reflect this Light in the dark world, so that others too may come to the Light. Isaiah is so bold as to prophesy, 'The Gentiles shall come to your light; and kings to the brightness of your rising' (Isa. 60:3). Paul, too, urges Christians to shine. Christians are to be different – contrary and counter to the sinful world: 'blameless and harmless, children of God without fault in the midst of a crooked and perverse generation, among whom you shine as lights in the world' (Phil. 2:15). Have you ever seen a phosphorescent light bulb? Such a bulb takes in light, and then, when darkness falls, emits the light. Having received the light of Christ, Christians are to emit the light of Christ – to be phosphorescent. Jesus Himself commands His disciples in all ages, 'Let your light so shine before men, that they may see your good works and glorify your Father in heaven' (Matt. 5:16). The world may be hostile to the Christian faith. But a life transformed by Christ and a life shining for Christ always makes an impact.

The Dawning of the Kingdom

In Proverbs 4:18, we read that 'the path of the just is like the shining sun, that shines ever brighter unto the perfect day.' Isaiah's prophecy describes the coming perfect day. In words taken up by John in Revelation, Isaiah foresaw the most glorious time for all God's redeemed when 'Your sun shall no longer go down, nor shall your moon withdraw itself; for the LORD will be your everlasting light, and the days of your mourning shall be ended' (Isa. 60:20).

Isaiah's prophecy concerns the time when every believer will truly 'Rise and shine.' The prophecy is a glimpse of the new heavens and the new earth – the cosmic consummation of our salvation which will be inaugurated when Christ comes again in glory to take His people to be with Him for ever. It is beyond our current comprehension. But we can say that it will be endless day and endless bliss.

Darkness in the Bible – as we have intimated – signifies sin, evil and condemnation. But in glory all this will have been eternally banished by God, for 'there shall be no night' (Rev. 22:5). Christians will be eternally saved and eternally safe in the nearer presence of God, in the city of the New Jerusalem. 'The city had no need of the sun or of the moon to shine in it, for the glory of God illuminated it. The Lamb is its light' (Rev. 21:23). Such a prospect awaits God's redeemed. We shall surely rise and shine! We will hear the words of Isaiah again, but in a much richer, fuller way: 'Arise, shine; for your light has come! And the glory of the LORD is risen upon you' (Isa. 60:1).

> *No need of the sunlight in heaven, we're told,*
> *The Light of the world is Jesus!*
> *The Lamb is the Light in the City of Gold,*
> *The Light of the world is Jesus!*

(PHILIPP P BLISS 1838–76)

33

'He couldn't lace his boots'

The expression 'He couldn't lace his boots' is used when one person is compared less favourably with another. Think, for instance, of the occasions when you meet an older man who is convinced that the football era of his youth was the greatest ever. He might say – with nostalgia – 'The players of today could not lace the boots of a George Best, Bobby Charlton, Nat Lofthouse, etc.' A wag once quipped, 'Nostalgia isn't what it used to be.' You sometimes meet people who are convinced that the music, sport, working-life, social conditions, etc., of the past were all far better than the present. Perhaps they have 'rose-tinted spectacles'. Ecclesiastes 7:10, though, reads pointedly: 'Say not, "Why were the former days better than these?" For it is not from wisdom that you ask this' (ESV). While we may be thankful for past mercies, undue disgruntlement with the present is ultimately disgruntlement with God's providence. We must repent if this is true of us …

The expression 'He couldn't lace his boots' is not found verbatim in the Bible. But the cultural equivalent is. John the Baptist was Jesus' forerunner. He prepared the way for the Messiah by his preaching. In proclaiming the coming Christ, John the Baptist announced: 'There comes One after me who is mightier than I, whose sandal strap I am not worthy to stoop down and loose' (Mark 1:7). According to Jesus, John the Baptist was the greatest prophet ever. He said of him, 'For I say to you, among those born of women there is not a greater prophet than John the Baptist' (Luke 7:28). Great man though John was, however, God gave him an insight into One who alone

143

could be described as truly 'great'. God gave John an insight into the Person of His own Son – the longed-for Messiah, who was about to begin His public ministry by being baptized in the Jordan by John.

Slaves and sandals

In Bible days, one task of a slave was to untie his master's shoes and wash his feet. John, though, was aware that Christ was so great that he was not worthy even to act as His lowly slave. He was not worthy even to stoop down and wash the feet of the Master. He thus confessed, 'There comes One after me who is mightier than I, whose sandal strap I am not worthy to stoop down and loose' (Mark 1:7). John, then, was saying the cultural equivalent of 'He couldn't lace his boots.' He was declaring the supreme, incomparable greatness of the Lord Jesus Christ.

Truth be told, no one can 'lace the boots' of the Lord Jesus. The great and prominent personalities, princes and politicians of this world fade into insignificance when compared with Him. He is the eternal Son of God. He is the second person of the Trinity. He came into the world to save sinners. He lived and spoke like no one else. He died and rose again to procure the salvation of His people. He is the only Saviour. He ascended back to heaven and is enthroned at God's right hand. One day He is coming back to earth in power and great glory, and every knee shall bow and pay homage to King Jesus. There is none like Christ. The greatest person on earth cannot 'lace the boots' of the eternal Son of God. His greatness is not a comparative one but a superlative one.

The following, anonymously written tract is fittingly entitled *The Incomparable Christ.* We quote it, as it brings out something of the wonder of the One whom John knew, whose sandals he was not worthy to untie:

'He couldn't lace his boots'

Jesus, the Christ, born of a virgin some 2,000 years ago, was raised in obscurity.

He possessed neither wealth nor high social standing. His relatives were inconspicuous, and He had neither training nor formal education. In infancy He startled a king; in childhood He puzzled doctors; in manhood He ruled the course of nature, walked upon the billows as if pavements, and hushed the sea to sleep.

He healed the multitudes without medicine and made no charge for His service.

He never wrote a book, and yet many times more books have been written about Him than about anyone else who has ever lived. His discourses and teaching have been translated into over 1,000 languages, and have a circulation many times greater than that of any other writing in existence.

He never wrote a song, and yet He has furnished the theme for more songs than all the songwriters combined.

He never founded a college, but all the schools put together cannot boast of having as many students.

He never marshalled an army, nor drafted a soldier, nor fired a gun; and yet no leader ever had more volunteers who have, under His orders, made more rebels stack arms and surrender without a shot fired.

He never practised psychiatry, and yet He has healed more broken hearts than all the doctors far and near.

Once each week the wheels of commerce cease their turning and multitudes wend their way to worshipping assemblies to pay homage and respect to Him.

The names of the past proud statesmen of Greece and Rome have come and gone. The names of past scientists, philosophers and theologians have come and gone, but the name of this man abounds more and more. Though time has spread over 2,000 years between the people of this generation, and the scene of His crucifixion, He still lives. Herod could not destroy Him, and the grave could not hold Him. God raised Him from the dead.

He stands forth upon the highest pinnacle of heavenly glory, proclaimed by God, acknowledged by angels, adored by saints, and feared by devils, as the living, personal Christ, our Lord and Saviour.

34

'Thus far and no further'

As a boy, I was infatuated with the professional wrestling on the TV, with its mix of theatre, drama, athleticism, seeming brutality and farce. At times, it seemed to have a formula. There would be a 'heel', that is, a 'bad guy/villain' against a 'blue eye', that is, a handsome 'good guy' who wrestled cleanly. The villain – much to the chagrin of the very vocal audience – would seem to 'get away with murder' by breaking the rules. Eventually, though, after repeated warnings from the referee and to the joy of the crowd, the 'heel' would get disqualified, and the 'blue eye' would be declared the winner. The referee's patience at the villain's rule-bending eventually ran out. It was a case of 'thus far and no further'.

In Job 38:8 (and the following verses), Almighty God speaks and asks some rhetorical questions about His creation and continual supervision of the world. He states, 'Who shut in the sea with doors … and prescribed limits for it and set bars and doors, and said, "Thus far shall you come, and no farther, and here shall your proud waves be stayed"?' (ESV). Another love of mine is the south Wales coast. It is so good to go down to the sea and watch the tide roll in. But why are there limits to the tide? Why doesn't the sea continue to come in and eventually overwhelm the land? Our verses from Job tell us. It is because Almighty God has set its limits. He has His prescribed boundaries. 'Thus far shall you come, and no farther, and here shall your proud waves be stayed.'

But can we consider God's ordained physical boundaries in a spiritual sense as well? I believe we can.

Eternal Salvation

We can think of God's boundaries in relation to our eternal salvation. According to the Bible, we are born in a perilous state. We are born sinners and thus liable to the wrath of God. But why does God not let us continue in that state? Because He has His merciful boundaries. He has ordained the days of both our first and second birth. Those chosen in Christ in eternity past will surely come to faith in Christ in time. God has fixed the boundary of their unbelief and ordained the day of their salvation. The working of His Spirit will ensure that they are convicted of their sin and lost plight and drawn to the crucified Saviour for full salvation.

As an example of this, think of the Apostle Paul. He was vehemently and violently opposed to the Christian faith. God allowed this to continue. Saul (as he was then known) persecuted the Christian church. Then, at the appointed time, on the road to Damascus, he had a life-changing encounter with the glorified Christ. God had set a boundary to his unbelief. 'Thus far … and no farther.'

Earthly Suffering

We can think of God's prescribed boundaries in relation to the suffering everyone will experience in this life to a greater or lesser degree. The world in which we live is perilous and precarious. Any one of us could experience the sudden loss of our health, our job or a loved one. Suffering seems so random and heartless – but not for the Christian. God has His hand on our life. He has promised that there will be a boundary to our suffering. He will tailor our suffering for our benefit. If we never had any trials or suffering, we would perhaps lose our sense of dependence on God, and get too comfortable and complacent in this world.

But if our trials were so severe, we might be tempted to doubt the love and wisdom of God. So God tailors our suffering by His providence. First Corinthians 10:13 assures us: 'God is faithful, who will not allow you to be tempted [that is, tested] beyond what you are able, but with the temptation [that is, test] will also make the way of escape, that you may be able to bear it.'

As we have seen, our suffering will not be without length, but borne 'thus far ... and no further'. If we belong to Jesus, God will either tailor our circumstances or give us grace to live within the boundaries of the circumstances He has ordained. In 2 Corinthians 12:9, He promises, 'My grace is sufficient for you.' If God sends us on stony paths, He will provide us with strong shoes.

Exquisite Splendour

Finally, the Bible assures us that the very day of our death is not accidental but providential. Our life on earth is a case of God pronouncing, 'Thus far shall you come, and no farther.' 'In Your book they all were written, the days fashioned for me, when as yet there were none of them' (Ps. 139:16). 'He ... has determined their preappointed times and the boundaries of their dwellings' (Acts 17:26).

So our ultimate and supreme comfort is to know that Almighty God is in absolute sovereign control over all things. He is too loving to be unkind and too wise to make mistakes. The waves of the sea are far mightier than we are, but God has put a limit on them, saying, 'Thus far shall you come, and no farther, and here shall your proud waves be stayed.' And God's boundaries also apply to our time of unbelief, the sufferings we undergo and even the exact number of days we will live on earth. The God of the Bible 'works all things according to the counsel of His will'

(Eph. 1:11). Knowing Him as our loving, heavenly Father through Jesus Christ His Son, we are encouraged to trust Him day by day, and praise Him in and through whatever He sees fit to send our way. In summary, with God's prescribed boundaries in mind, we may rejoice and say:

> *Sov'reign Ruler of the skies,*
> *Ever gracious, ever wise;*
> *All my times are in Thy hand,*
> *All events at Thy command.*
>
> *His decrees, who formed the earth,*
> *Fixed my first and second birth;*
> *Parents, native place and time,*
> *All appointed were by Him.*
>
> *He that formed me in the womb,*
> *He shall guide me to the tomb;*
> *All my times shall ever be*
> *Ordered by His wise decree.*
>
> *Times of sickness, times of health,*
> *Times of penury and wealth;*
> *Times of trial and of grief,*
> *Times of triumph and relief.*
>
> *Plagues and death around me fly;*
> *Till He bids I cannot die;*
> *Not a single shaft can hit,*
> *Till the God of love sees fit.*

(JOHN RYLAND, 1753–1825)

35

Holding out an olive branch

To 'hold out an olive branch' refers to an offer of peace and conciliation. Picture an occasion when two people or two parties are at odds with each other over some difference or grievance. It is getting nasty. One side, though, decides that the state of conflict and animosity is not good. This being so, perhaps through a middle party or mediator, a possible resolution to the conflict is suggested. When this is done, they 'hold out an olive branch' to the other side. The 'olive branch' – that is, the terms of peace – is accepted, and the conflict is resolved and harmony is restored. The olive branch has become a well-known symbol of peace.

The Universal Flood

The origins of the term 'holding out an olive branch' are very ancient. It originates from the time of Noah, and Noah was born in the tenth generation after Adam the first man. In the days of Noah, 'the world that then existed perished, being flooded with water' (2 Pet. 3:6). That is, God sent a universal flood to destroy the world He had made. The historical account of all this is recorded for us in Genesis 6–8. Sin had entered the world and it grew worse and worse, provoking the judgment of God against it. The inspired account informs us:

'The LORD saw that the wickedness of man was great in the earth, and that every intent of the thoughts of his heart was only evil continually. And the LORD was sorry that He had made man on the earth, and He was grieved in His heart. So the LORD said, "I will destroy man whom I have created from the face of the earth, both man and beast, creeping thing and birds of the air, for I am sorry that I have made them"' (Gen. 6:5-7). God was true to

His Word, and, by means of a flood, did indeed blot out the world He had made.

By the grace of God, however, Noah and his family were saved from the literal and metaphorical floods of God's wrath. The flood came with a vengeance, but 'By faith Noah, being divinely warned of things not yet seen, moved with godly fear, prepared an ark for the saving of his household ...' (Heb. 11:7). Noah took his family into the ark – along with selected animals and provisions – and so was saved from the judgment of God. In the ark, he literally 'rode out' the judgment of God until it had abated and accomplished its goal.

After forty tumultuous days, the flood did eventually begin to abate. The waters of judgment receded. Noah sent a dove out of the ark to 'test the waters'. The dove returned, an event suggesting that the world was still uninhabitable. Noah then tried this action again a week later. 'The dove came to him in the evening, and behold, a freshly plucked olive leaf was in her mouth; and Noah knew that the waters had receded from the earth' (Gen. 8:11). When Noah sent the dove out from the ark the next time, it did not return at all.

The Olive Branch

The freshly plucked olive leaf in the beak of the dove spoke loudly to Noah. It told him, 'The judgment is now over. Peace is now here. New life and new hope have arrived.' Olives, we are told, do not grow at high altitude. Hence, the olive leaf in the dove's beak was proof to Noah that the flood sent by God in judgment was over, and that the earth was safe and habitable once again.

Peace with God

In the light of the whole Bible, we have to say that the Lord Jesus Christ is God's 'olive branch'. Jesus holds out the offer of peace and new life to sinners under the judgment of God. Our sin alien-ates us from God and puts us under His condemnation. The gospel, however, declares that 'God was in Christ reconciling the world to Himself, not imputing their trespasses to them' (2 Cor. 5:19). On the cross, Christ endured the floods of divine judgment against sin. On the cross, He could say to God the Father: 'Your wrath lies heavy upon me, and You have afflicted me with all Your waves' (Ps. 88:7). Christ endured the floods of God's wrath to save the believer from it. He suffered the judgment of God to make our peace with God. Scripture tells of Jesus 'having made peace through the blood of His cross' (Col. 1:20). It is the blessed experience of every believer in Jesus to be able to affirm, 'Therefore, having been justified by faith, we have peace with God through our Lord Jesus Christ' (Rom. 5:1). Jesus is God's olive branch. If our faith is in Him, the judgment we deserve is over. We have eternal peace with God. We enjoy eternal life – fellowship with God our Maker, both here and hereafter.

In Christ, then, God holds out an olive branch to a con-demned world. The imperative responsibility of the sinner is to take it. 'Believe on the Lord Jesus Christ, and you will be saved' (Acts 16:31). 'Behold, now is the accepted time; behold, now is the day of salvation' (2 Cor. 6:2). Jesus is God's olive branch, and the cross of Christ is our ark of safety from the divine judgment we deserve.

> *The tempest's awful voice was heard,*
> *O Christ, it broke on Thee!*
> *Thy open bosom was my ward,*
> *It braved the storm for me.*
> *Thy form was scarred, Thy visage marred;*
> *Now cloudless peace for me.*

(ANNE ROSS COUSIN, 1824–1906)

36

A baptism of fire

We use the expression 'He underwent a baptism of fire' to describe a tough initiation. Every journey starts with a first step. Think of the nerves of a Premiership football referee when he officiates at his first Premiership game, heckled and jeered by forty thousand or more fans. What if he had no option but to send off a top player from the home team for a bad foul? Then the writer well remembers his first day as the sole ticket-master at a small but busy railway station. A long queue of impatient commuters gathered there early one Monday morning to buy their daily, weekly and monthly train tickets. A train then broke down up the line, causing the rail network to come to a grinding halt. Some of the paying public decided that their consequent lateness for work was all my fault, and took it out on me accordingly! My first shift at the railway station was 'a baptism of fire'. Or, to change the metaphor, I was 'thrown in at the deep end'.

When John the Baptist – Christ's 'forerunner' – preached and prophesied about the impending appearance of Christ on the earth, he foretold, 'He will baptize you with the Holy Spirit and with fire' (Luke 3:16). The prophecy came true and will yet come true. On the Day of Pentecost, the Lord Jesus poured out His Holy Spirit on the earth. The Holy Spirit came in the form of 'tongues, as of fire' (Acts 2:3). It is the Holy Spirit of Christ who imparts all the blessings of Christ's redeeming work to the human soul and makes the salvation He procured at Calvary effectual in an individual's life. While Christ procured our salvation, it is the Holy Spirit who puts us into the actual possession of it. In the words of *The Westminster Shorter Catechism*, 'We are made partakers of the redemption purchased by Christ, by the effectual application of it to us by His Holy Spirit.'[1]

Fire, in the Bible, also speaks of judgment. This points us forward to the Last Judgment on the final Day when 'each one's work will become clear; for the Day will declare it, because it will be revealed by fire; and the fire will test each one's work, of what sort it is' (1 Cor. 3:13). This final judgment of the world will be undertaken by the Lord Jesus Christ, the Bible says, for God 'has appointed a day on which He will judge the world in righteousness by the Man whom He has ordained ...' (Acts 17:31). The thought of judgment naturally unsettles us. But – as John Calvin has written – 'It is an extraordinary comfort to us to know that the judgment is committed to the very one whose coming means, for us, nothing but salvation.'[2]

Calvary: The True Baptism of Fire

'He underwent a baptism of fire ...' The Lord Jesus underwent 'a baptism of fire' like none other. He left heaven for earth for the sole purpose of undergoing this baptism, and lived the whole of His life in its shadow. Speaking of His coming death at Calvary, He said, 'I have a baptism to be baptized with, and how distressed I am till it is accomplished!' (Luke 12:50). Calvary was truly a 'baptism of fire' beyond compare. Jesus asked James and John the rhetorical question: 'Are you able to drink the cup that I drink, and be baptized with the baptism that I am baptized with?' (Mark 10:38).

On Calvary's cross, the sinless Christ was made accountable for His people's sins, and God poured out His holy wrath on Him

1. *The Westminster Shorter Catechism*, Question 29

2. John Calvin, *Truth for all Time*, trans.Stuart Ollyot, Banner of Truth Trust, Edinburgh, 1988, p. 43

in judgment to save His people from that judgment. On Calvary, Christ could say, 'Your wrath lies heavy upon me, and You have afflicted me with all your waves' (Ps. 88:7). A holy God can only punish every infraction of His holy law. On Calvary's cross, Christ was punished in place of His people, bearing their penalty for breaking God's law, and thus saving them from the eternal curse of breaking that law. 'Christ has redeemed us from the curse of the law, having become a curse for us (for it is written, "Cursed is everyone who hangs on a tree")' (Gal. 3:13).

Calvary, therefore, was Christ's 'baptism of fire'. There He suffered the fires of God's judgment, and, in suffering so, He extinguished those flames for all who put their faith in Him. He experienced the fires of God's wrath and, in doing so, has eternally saved every believer from that wrath, praise His Name. 'We have peace with God through our Lord Jesus Christ' (Rom. 5:1). Calvary was Christ's 'baptism of fire'.

> *Jehovah bade His sword awake,*
> *O Christ, it woke 'gainst Thee!*
> *Thy blood the flaming blade must slake,*
> *Thy heart its sheath must be!*
> *All for my sake, my peace to make,*
> *Now sleeps that sword for me!*

> (ANNE ROSS COUSIN, 1824–1906)

37

Entering the lion's den

We use the expression 'Entering the lion's den' to refer to going into a hostile territory or environment where we fear we might get 'eaten alive'. In the U.K., the Secretary of State for Health 'entered the lion's den' when he went to speak at a nurses' conference and tried to explain that N.H.S. spending could not be limitless in the economic climate of the time. He was subject to slow handclapping as he spoke, and some walked out. A boxer 'enters the lion's den' when he boxes in his opponent's hometown and his opponent has the majority support of the crowd. Football supporters also use the term 'entering the lion's den' when they support their team at away games, and are heavily outnumbered by the home crowd.

While we use the expression 'entering the lion's den' in a metaphorical sense, Daniel 6 describes a time when the prophet Daniel was thrown into an actual den of lions. The historical background to this is as follows:

Daniel in the lion's den

Daniel had been exiled from the land of Israel to pagan Babylon. He was, by this time, an aged man, and Babylon was ruled by King Darius the Mede. Those in power wished to 'get one over' on Daniel – his godly character grated on them. Conniving together, they set things up so that 'whoever petitions any god or man for thirty days, except you, O king [Darius], shall be cast into the den of lions' (Dan. 6:7).

Daniel, being a man of God, was a model, law-abiding citizen. Here, however, the law of the land clashed with the law of God, so he had no choice but to rebel against the earthly authority and obey the Higher Authority. He carried on just as he had always done: 'He went home. And in his upper room, with his windows open toward Jerusalem, he knelt down on his knees three times that day, and prayed and gave thanks before his God, as was his custom since early days' (Dan. 6:10). The consequence of Daniel's faithfulness to the true God was severe. The law of the land was applied 'and they brought Daniel and cast him into the den of lions' (Dan. 6:16).

But this was not the end of Daniel! God performed a miracle and saved His servant from being devoured by the lions. He caused them to act contrary to their nature. It was as if Daniel was in the company of kittens! When King Darius called to him the next day, fully expecting a dead silence, to his shock, he heard Daniel's voice. He was alive and well! Daniel testified, 'My God sent His angel and shut the lions' mouths, so that they have not hurt me …' (Dan. 6:22). The record continues and concludes: 'So Daniel was taken up out of the den, and no injury whatever was found on him, because he believed in his God' (Dan. 6:23). The story ends with a great change coming over King Darius. He realized that, although he was technically a king, there is a true King – the King of heaven, the one and only God. Darius then bowed before Him and made the confession: '… the God of Daniel … He is the living God, and steadfast forever; His kingdom is the one which shall not be destroyed, and His dominion shall endure to the end. He delivers and rescues, and He works signs and wonders in heaven and on earth, who has delivered Daniel from the power of the lions' (Dan. 6:26, 27).

The Absolute Sovereignty of God

What do we learn from 'Daniel in the lion's den?' There are many matters, but consider two.

First of all, note that we are immortal until our work is done and God's purposes for us on earth are fulfilled. Humanly speaking, Daniel should have met an instant death in the lion's den. But God had other plans. God preserved him. He had more work for Daniel to do on earth. It is good to remember that the date and time of our deaths are all written in the divine diary. We will not die prematurely, before God's time – and we will not linger a moment on earth after His time, either. God knows best.

Secondly, 'Daniel in the lion's den' reminds us that our God is in absolute and total control of all things. He is in charge of both the sparrow that cheeps and the lion that roars. He is in charge of all the details of our lives – pleasant and hostile. The technical term for this is 'divine providence'. Nothing happens 'by chance'. All has been foreordained and prearranged by our loving Father in heaven. He has His eternal plan.

> *'The decrees of God are His eternal purpose, according to the counsel of His will, whereby, for His own glory, He hath foreordained whatsoever comes to pass.'*

> *'God's works of providence are His most holy, wise and powerful preserving and governing all His creatures and all their actions.'[1]*

And what of us when we enter our lesser 'lion's dens'? For example, consider difficulties at work, stress at home and even awkward people in the church. Daniel's experience is a reminder that God is in control. He is on the throne, so all is ultimately well. 'The LORD has established His throne in heaven, and His kingdom rules over all' (Ps. 103:19). Scripture affirms 'We know that for those who love God all things work together for good ...'

---

1. *The Westminster Shorter Catechism,* Questions 7 and 11

(Rom. 8:28, ESV) and our present difficulties and even hostilities are no exceptions to this all-embracing rule.

Under God's good providence, therefore, even the 'lions' around us are working for our ultimate blessing. They might well be hostile to us and have evil intentions. But we are to look beyond them. We look to our sovereign God and loving heavenly Father and 'If God is for us, who can be against us …' (Rom. 8:31, ESV). Let us then 'Dare to be a Daniel'. Let us be faithful to God through thick and thin. He will keep us from harm in the lion's den! And one day, if we belong to Jesus, He will take us out of the lion's den to dwell in the safety of His nearer presence for all eternity.

38

A leopard doesn't change its spots

The expression 'A leopard doesn't change its spots' is usually used ruefully. Perhaps you recall a classmate from the primary school who was known for his ability to steal sweets from a shop near the school. Then you notice in the local paper that, as an adult, the same person has been jailed for stealing cars. 'A leopard doesn't change its spots.' The expressions means something like 'Human nature is human nature. Human nature does not change. Some people act very predictably according to their nature. They are like they are.'

Our expression concerning the leopard and its spots is a biblical one. It was actually used by God Himself when He spoke through His servant Jeremiah. In a passage containing many indictments against His people, God said to the prophet in Jeremiah 13:23: 'Can the Ethiopian change his skin or the leopard its spots? Then may you also do good who are accustomed to do evil.'

The Human Condition
Sadly, the full verse from which our expression is taken is a biblical diagnosis of the human condition. On a positive note, though, a correct diagnosis always precedes a cure. The Bible's diagnosis of us is that we are sinners by nature. It is not so much sinning that makes us sinners, but rather that we sin because we *are* sinners. In and of ourselves, we can no more alter this than an Ethiopian can change his skin colour or a leopard can

change its spots. David confessed, 'Behold, I was brought forth in iniquity, and in sin my mother conceived me' (Ps. 51:5). And the Lord Jesus taught, 'A good tree cannot bear bad fruit, nor can a bad tree bear good fruit' (Matt. 7:18). It is because we are 'bad trees' that we bring forth 'bad fruit'.

Our sin would not be a problem for us if God were not God. He is holy and just, and as such can only punish sin. Sin is thus our worst problem of all, because we cannot do anything to change our sinful nature. 'Can the Ethiopian change his skin or the leopard its spots? Then may you also do good who are accustomed to do evil.'

The Bible teaches the 'total depravity' of human nature, that is, that sin has affected us totally. Sin has affected and infected all our faculties – our thinking, motives, desires and will, as well as our actions. By nature, we will not seek or desire God. A sinner no more seeks God than a criminal seeks a magistrate. We have lost the ability to please God. We are unable to save ourselves from our sinful, condemned condition. We cannot 'pull ourselves up by our own bootlaces'.

> *Man, by his fall into sin, hath wholly lost all ability of will to any spiritual good accompanying salvation, so as a natural man, being altogether averse from that good, and dead in sin, is not able, by his own strength, to convert himself or prepare himself thereunto.*[1]

The Human Conversion

Is our condition therefore totally helpless and hopeless? It would be, were it not for the saving grace of God. It would be apart from the gracious ministry of the Holy Spirit in our lives. God is able to do what we cannot do. He has provided helpless, hopeless sinners with a salvation. And this salvation is very thorough.

---

1. *The Westminster Confession of Faith,* Chapter 9, Paragraph 3

It is a matter of redemption both accomplished and applied. It was accomplished by Christ at Calvary, when He suffered the condemnation due to sinners. It is applied to individual human hearts by the Holy Spirit of God. He does not leave us to our own devices. He enables, assists and ensures that we partake of Christ, and so are fully saved from our dreadful and damnable human condition. Almighty God is actually able to change our nature, so that, instead of running away from Him, we are drawn to Him, and enabled to partake of the salvation He has provided for us in Christ:

> *All those whom God hath predestined unto life, and those only, He is pleased, in His appointed and accepted time, effectually to call, by His Word and Spirit, out of that state of sin and death, in which they are by nature, to grace and salvation, by Jesus Christ; enlightening their minds spiritually and savingly to understand the things of God, taking away their heart of stone, and giving unto them a heart of flesh; renewing their wills, and, by His almighty power, determining them to that which is good, and effectually drawing them to Jesus Christ; yet so, as they come most freely, being made willing by His grace.*

> *This effectual call is of God's free and special grace alone, not from anything at all foreseen in man, who is altogether passive therein, until, being quickened and renewed by the Holy Spirit, he is thereby enabled to answer this call, and to embrace the grace offered and conveyed in it.[2]*

'A leopard doesn't change its spots.' Likewise, we cannot change our human nature. But God can! Salvation is a matter of saving and transforming grace. 'Therefore, if anyone is in Christ, he is a new creation …' (2 Cor. 5:17). God's indictment through Jeremiah was that we cannot do good because we are evil at the core. But grace transforms us from the inside out. One piece of evidence of saving

---

2. *The Westminster Confession of Faith,* Chapter 10, Paragraphs 1 and 2

grace received is the desire to please God. This desire, though, is not to earn our salvation, but rather to express our gratitude for the salvation we have received. 'By this we know that we know Him, if we keep His commandments' (1 John 2:3). 'No one born of God commits sin; for God's nature abides in him, and he cannot sin because he is born of God' (1 John 3:9, RSV). Occasional lapses apart, the thrust of our life now is to please our Father in heaven.

'A leopard doesn't change its spots' for sure. Human nature is what it is. But who are we to say who is or who is not beyond divine redemption – that is, beyond the saving, transforming grace of God? There is a gospel of grace!

How sad our state by nature is!
Our sin how deep its stains!
And Satan binds our captive minds
Fast in his slavish chains.

But there's a voice of sovereign grace
Sounds from the sacred Word;
Ho! Ye despairing sinners, come
And trust upon the Lord!

My soul obeys the Almighty's call
And runs to this relief;
I would believe Thy promise, Lord,
O help my unbelief!

To the dear fountain of Thy blood,
Incarnate God, I fly;
Here let me wash my guilty soul
From crimes of deepest dye.

A guilty, weak and helpless wretch,
On Thy kind arms I fall!
Be Thou my strength and righteousness,
My Jesus and my all!

(ISAAC WATTS, 1674–1748)

39

As old as the hills

The expression 'as old as the hills' is self-explanatory. I was born and bred by the side of a range of mountains in south Wales. These mountains were there years before I was around, and, if the Lord tarries, they will also be there for years after I have left the scene of earth and time.

While the expression 'as old as the hills' is not found in the Bible, it does yet give us a handle into the nature of the God revealed in the Bible. The hills are immense and unchanging. The God of the Bible is almighty, eternal, unchangeable and dependable. In Psalm 90:2, we read: 'Before the mountains were brought forth, or ever You had formed the earth and the world, even from everlasting to everlasting, You are God.' The God of the Bible predates even the ancient hills. He is eternal. He is the uncreated Creator who has neither beginning nor end.

> *Before the hills in order stood,*
> *Or earth received her frame,*
> *From everlasting Thou art God,*
> *To endless years the same.*

> (ISAAC WATTS, 1674–1748)

The Presence of God

An obvious point about the hills is that they are there. A basic point about the God of the Bible is that He is there also. Only 'The fool has said in his heart, "There is no God"' (Ps. 14:1). God is. He is the God 'Who is and who was and who is to come' (Rev. 1:4). The Psalmist wrote, 'As the mountains surround Jerusalem, so the LORD surrounds His people from this time forth and forever'

(Ps. 125:2). David testified: 'I have set the LORD always before me; because He is at my right hand I shall not be moved' (Ps. 16:8).

The Power of God

The hills and mountains dwarf us with their age and size. Life itself can also dwarf us. It can present us with great difficulties – difficulties greater than we are. It presents us with slopes that are steep and hard, and mountainous problems that seem impossible to move and overcome. What do we do when we find ourselves facing a 'mountain' that is greater than we are? The Christian response is to turn to God. In Psalm 97:5, we read: 'The mountains melt like wax at the presence of the LORD, at the presence of the Lord of the whole earth.' This reminds us that the Lord God is greater than all our mountainous problems and has the solution to all our difficulties. Through prayer we may 'tap into' His omnipotence and know the all-sufficiency of His grace for whatever our need may be. Faith can move mountains only because God Himself can move mountains. The Lord Jesus had this in mind when He encouraged His disciples in prayer with the exhortation: 'Have faith in God. For assuredly, I say to you, whoever says to this mountain, "Be removed and be cast into the sea," and does not doubt in his heart, but believes that those things he says will be done, he will have whatever he says. Therefore I say to you, whatever things you ask when you pray, believe that you receive them, and you will have them' (Mark 11:22 ff.).

The Provision of God

Genesis 22 contains the account of Abraham's near-sacrifice of his son, Isaac. The story takes place on a mountain – Mount

168

Moriah. It draws to an end relating that 'Abraham called the name of the place The-LORD-Will-Provide; as it is said to this day "In the Mount of the LORD it shall be provided"' (Gen. 22:14). The Lord God did, indeed, provide for Abraham on Mount Moriah. He provided a ram to die in place of Isaac his son. God's provision here thus spared Isaac's life, as well as sparing Abraham from suffering much pain and sorrow.

God's provision on Mount Moriah was a foreshadowing of a Greater Provision He was to make in order to save sinners in the fullness of time when 'He … did not spare His own Son, but delivered Him up for us all' (Rom. 8:32). Some two thousand years after Abraham, Jesus died at Calvary. Calvary is located on the same ridge as Mount Moriah. Isaac asked his father the question, 'Where is the lamb for a burnt offering?' (Gen. 22:7). Abraham replied, 'My son, God will provide for Himself the lamb for a burnt offering' (Gen. 22:8). Abraham's words were prophetic. Two thousand years later, John the Baptist pointed to Jesus and said, 'Behold! The Lamb of God who takes away the sin of the world!' (John 1:29).

The death of Christ at Calvary is God's Ultimate Provision. Jesus is God's provision of the Saviour we so desperately need. Just as Isaac was spared because God provided a ram to die in his stead, so, likewise, those who trust in Jesus and His substitutionary death are spared – saved and spared from eternal punishment. As the saying goes, 'For God cannot demand a payment twice, first at Jesus' hand and then again at mine.' Because God did not spare His own Son, sinners who believe in Jesus are eternally spared.

Calvary then was God's mount of provision. There, in His Son, He provided eternal salvation for all who believe:

A Little Bird Told Me

One day they led Him up Calvary's mountain,
One day they nailed Him to die on a tree;
Suffering anguish, despised and rejected,

Bearing our sins, my Redeemer is He!

(J WILBUR CHAPMAN, 1859–1918)

'As old as the hills'. We look up to the hills. They are high, mighty, solid and unchanging and old. The hills are a silent reminder to the believer to look up! Look up to God, our all-sufficient maker, sustainer and Saviour. 'I will lift up my eyes to the hills – from whence comes my help? My help comes from the LORD, who made heaven and earth' (Ps. 121:1, 2).

40

Doubting Thomas

A 'Doubting Thomas' refers to someone who is sceptical about a matter. From time to time – especially during the 'silly season' when news is short – the papers report sightings of 'the Loch Ness monster' in Loch Ness, Scotland. 'Nessie' – as the monster is known – certainly brings in the tourists. The local souvenir shops have a brisk trade in selling plastic-model 'Nessies' for the mantelpiece. But does Nessie actually exist in reality? I confess that I for one am a sceptic. When it comes to the Loch Ness monster, I'm something of a 'Doubting Thomas'.

Thomas's Doubts

The Bible tells us of a man who initially doubted that the Lord Jesus had risen from the dead. His name was Thomas. Thomas was one of the twelve chosen disciples, and it is from him that we get the description a 'Doubting Thomas'. John's Gospel records three appearances of the risen Christ to the disciples, and after the first resurrection appearance of Christ to them, John relates the following:

'Thomas, called the Twin, one of the twelve, was not with them when Jesus came. The other disciples therefore said to him, "We have seen the LORD." So he said to them, "Unless I see in His hands the print of the nails, and put my finger into the print of the nails, and put my hand into His side, I will not believe"' (John 20:24, 25).

The Bible, then, is a very candid Book. It is very honest about the faults, failures and even doubts of the followers of Jesus. Thomas is one such case. Why was he missing from the gathering of the disciples? We don't know. We do know, though, that he has gone down in history as being famous for what he did not believe! None of the disciples were incredulous. Hardened fishermen that many of them were, they would only believe and proclaim the risen Christ if Christ had, in fact, risen. What, though, happened to Thomas's scepticism? John tells us:

'And after eight days His disciples were again inside, and Thomas with them. Jesus came, the doors being shut, and stood in the midst, and said, "Peace to you!" Then He said to Thomas, "Reach your finger here, and look at My hands; and reach your hand here, and put it into My side. Do not be unbelieving, but believing." And Thomas answered and said to Him, "My Lord and my God!" Jesus said to him, "Thomas, because you have seen Me, you have believed. Blessed are those who have not seen and yet have believed"' (John 20:26-29).

Thomas's Deliverance

Here, then, we see Thomas's doubts being quashed and quelled in an instant. The risen Christ met him. For Thomas, seeing was believing. The evidence that he sought was given to him, and so he worshipped the crucified but risen Saviour. 'My Lord and my God!' he confessed. And with this declaration and confession of Thomas, John's Gospel reaches a climax. The absolute deity of Christ is a distinctive feature of John's Gospel, and the resurrection of Christ from the dead is the final proof and lynchpin of that deity.

It was Christ's real, bodily resurrection that convinced Thomas of Christ's absolute deity. Jesus Christ is God! And so Thomas worshipped Him. Only God is to be worshipped, yet Christ accepted Thomas's worship of Him. He did not rebuke him for idolatry. It shows that the risen Christ is God – the Son of God and God the Son – 'declared to be the Son of God with power, according to the Spirit of holiness, by the resurrection from the dead' (Rom. 1:4).

Thomas's Descendants

You and I, of course, are not in Thomas's position in that we are unable to see the risen Christ with our physical eyes. But according to the Bible, our experience of Christ can be just as real as Thomas's when we 'see' Him with the eyes of faith. Amazingly, the Bible teaches that if our faith is in Christ, our blessedness is actually equal to Thomas's. If we believe in Jesus, Jesus actually pronounces His blessing upon us. John concludes his account of Thomas's encounter with the risen Christ with the following words of the Lord Jesus to Thomas and to us today: 'Jesus said to him, "Thomas, because you have seen Me, you have believed. Blessed are those who have not seen and yet have believed"' (John 20:29). The same thought was taken up by Peter many years later when he wrote, 'Whom having not seen you love. Though now you do not see Him, yet believing, you rejoice with joy inexpressible and full of glory, receiving the end of your faith – the salvation of your souls' (1 Pet. 1:8, 9).

Doubting Thomas. The grace of God in Christ, however, dispelled Thomas's doubts. And by the miracle of God's grace, many doubting Thomases since Thomas's day have also come to know that Christ has risen indeed. He is a living Saviour who 'walks with me, and talks with me, along life's narrow way.'

> *That night the apostles met in fear,*
> *Amidst them came their Lord most dear,*
> *And said 'My peace be on all here.' Alleluia!*
>
> *When Thomas first the tidings heard,*
> *How they had seen the risen Lord,*
> *He doubted the disciples' word! Alleluia!*

A Little Bird Told Me

'My pierced side, O Thomas, see,
My hands, my feet I show to thee,
Not faithless but believing be!' Alleluia!

No longer Thomas then denied;
He saw the feet, the hands the side;
'Thou art my Lord and God!' he cried. Alleluia!

How blest are they who have not seen,
And yet whose faith has constant been!
For they eternal life shall win! Alleluia!

(ANON.)

'Almighty and everlasting God, who for the more confirmation of the faith did allow the Apostle Thomas to be doubtful of Thy Son's resurrection. Grant us so perfectly, and without all doubt, to believe in Thy Son Jesus Christ, that our faith in Thy sight may never be reproved …'[1]

---

1. *Saint Thomas the Apostle – The Collect,* From *The Book of Common Prayer*

41

'I'm at my wits' end'

To be at your wits' end is a highly unpleasant and undesirable experience. We use the expression 'I'm at my wits' end' to describe our condition when we find ourselves in a difficult, stressful circumstance with no apparent way out. We are at our wits' end. We fear that we are about to 'crack up' completely. Expressions with a similar meaning include 'I'm at the end of my tether' and 'I feel as though I've been boxed into a corner.' To 'have your wits about you', on the other hand, refers to being mentally alert and in charge. But to be at your wits' end refers to being utterly confused and perplexed, when a troublesome occasion or occurrence is beyond your intelligence and ability to solve and cope with.

The Saying's Origin
It is not very well known that the expression concerning our 'wits' end' is taken from the Bible – from Psalm 107 to be specific. In Psalm 107, we read of some sailors at sea who were caught up in a terrifying storm. The storm had them completely at its mercy. They were powerless to master it and in danger of losing their lives by shipwreck and drowning. The sailors were brought to their wits' end. The hand of Almighty God, though, was in it all. Taking up the poetic narrative, we read in Psalm 107:23 ff.

'They that go down to the sea in ships, that do business in great waters; these see the works of the LORD, and His wonders in the deep. For He commandeth, and raiseth the stormy wind, which lifteth up the waves thereof. They mount up to the heaven, they go down again to the depths: their soul is melted because of trouble. They reel to and fro, and stagger like a drunken man, *and are at their wits' end*' (KJV, emphasis mine).

The story, though, had a happy ending. Almighty God was superintending it all. The great Creator was in control of His creation. The sailors turned to Him, and in His mercy He intervened and alleviated their lost, distressed plight:

'Then they cry unto the LORD in their trouble, and He bringeth them out of their distresses. He maketh the storm a calm, so that the waves thereof are still. Then are they glad because they be quiet; so He bringeth them unto their desired haven' (Ps. 107:28-30, KJV).

The Saying's Application

What a wonderful lesson this gives to you and me! We have a God to whom we can turn when we are at our wits' end. He laughs at impossibilities. Our extremity is His opportunity. Our human impotence is not a problem to His divine omnipotence. God is greater than all our difficulties and problems! God has the solution to all our difficulties and problems. Through Christ, we have access to Him. By prayer we are privileged to be able to 'tap into' His infinite resources, when our resources have run out:

> *Got any rivers you think are uncrossable?*
> *Got any mountains you can't tunnel through?*
> *God specializes in things thought impossible*
> *And He can do what no other can do*

(OSCAR C. ELIASON, CIRCA 1945)

Scripture affirms, 'We know that for those who love God all things work together for good, for those who are called according to his purpose' (Rom. 8:28, ESV). So, does it mean that being brought to our wits' end is an exception to the 'all things' of this verse? Certainly not! 'All things' means what it says: '*all* things'. We may think of this in relation to two matters: the matter of salvation and the matter of suffering.

Salvation

Salvation is the greatest blessing we can ever or will ever receive. Before we experience the joy of salvation, though, God brings us to our wits' end. His Holy Spirit convicts us of our sin and condemnation. We realize we are undone and heading for hell. We realize that we are powerless to save ourselves – to blot out our sins and achieve a righteousness which fits us for heaven. But, as with the sailors in Psalm 107, the story does not end there. When we realize our need for a Saviour, God shows us the Saviour for our need, and bestows on us saving faith in Him. We call on the name of the Lord and are saved! The Lord Jesus is the all-sufficient Saviour for our need. His death for our sins has pacified the wrath of God. His righteousness, imputed to us, fits us for glory. Hallelujah!

Suffering

In Acts 14:22 we read, 'We must through many tribulations enter the kingdom of God.' It is doubtful whether we will ever meet a Christian who is exempt from suffering in this life. In His all-wise providence, God may see fit to bring us to our wits' end. Why? There is no short answer. But the answer of Paul in 2 Corinthians is that God brings us to our wits' end to draw us closer to Himself – to knock away our human props and self-sufficiency, and make us depend on Him all the more. In 2 Corinthians 1:8 and 9, Paul relates how he and his fellow workers in the gospel 'were burdened beyond measure, above strength, so that we despaired even of life. Yes, we had the sentence of death in ourselves, that we should not trust in ourselves but in God who raises the dead.'

Ease is agreeable, but ease has its perils. There is always a danger of spiritual complacency. God may thus see fit to 'stir up the nest' in His dealings with His children. Sanctified suffering makes us realize afresh our total dependence on God – His grace, His providence, His strength, His enabling. Suffering gives reality and urgency to our prayers. Our inadequacy is an opportunity to prove His total adequacy. Our insufficiency is an opportunity to prove His all-sufficiency. His promise is 'My grace is sufficient for you' (2 Cor. 12:9).

So remember those sailors in Psalm 107. They were 'at their wits' end'. But they cried to the Lord in their trouble, and He delivered them from their distress. When you are at your wits' end, God will not fail you either, for He has not changed. He is still a God of saving and sustaining grace.

> *When we have exhausted our store of endurance,*
> *When our strength has failed ere the day is half done,*
> *When we reach the end of our hoarded resources,*
> *Our Father's full giving is only begun.*
>
> *His love has no limit, His grace has no measure,*
> *His power has no boundary known unto men;*
> *For out of His infinite riches in Jesus,*
> *He giveth, and giveth, and giveth again!*

(ANNIE JOHNSON FLINT, 1861–1932)

42

Going the second mile

To 'go the second mile' refers to serving above and beyond the call of duty or what we are strictly obliged to do. The writer recalls how, when he worked for the railways, a female guard – Wendy – once accompanied an elderly gentleman on his journey back to his home in Bristol. She did this after she had completed her full shift and was about to go home herself. She was not paid for doing what she did. She did it solely out of kindness and a concern for a senior citizen's welfare. Going beyond the call of duty, she 'went the second mile'. (As it happened, her kindness became known, and she was given an 'Exceptional Service Award' by the company.)

The Background

The expression 'to go the second mile' stems from some words of the Lord Jesus Christ in the Sermon on the Mount. In Matthew 5:41, He exhorts His followers in these words: 'Whoever compels you to go one mile, go with him two.' The verb used here for 'compel' means 'to press into service'. The Lord Jesus lived and ministered during the Roman occupation of Israel. Soldiers from the Roman army were resented by the Jews because of racial and religious differences – even if the soldiers' presence did ensure a degree of peace, stability, law and order. Roman soldiers in Israel were quite at liberty to command a person to carry their pack or military equipment for a mile, thus sparing themselves the exertion. They could 'sequester' your service, and you would not argue with them. We witness an instance of this just before the Saviour's crucifixion at Calvary, where we read how the Roman soldiers 'press-ganged' Simon of Cyrene to carry Jesus' cross. 'Now as they came out, they found a man of Cyrene, Simon by name. Him they compelled to bear His cross' (Matt. 27:32).

A Roman soldier, then, was free to commandeer a non-Roman citizen to carry his heavy load for a mile. How glad you would be when you had covered the distance and could hand the weight back to him. But the Lord Jesus says that such a conscript should keep going! 'Whoever compels you to go one mile, go with him two.' Such a commandment would have brought gasps of astonishment from Jesus' original hearers, living in the Promised Land, but now occupied by a pagan power.

A Generous Spirit

We do not have soldiers on our streets compelling us to carry their load. But the spirit behind the command of the Lord Jesus to 'go the second mile' is still applicable. The Lord Jesus was inculcating generosity and a lavishly kind attitude in His followers, then and now. Christians are to be known for their generosity of spirit. This is not so that we may gain God's favour, but rather because we have been and are recipients of God's bounty and favour. Christians are recipients of the saving grace of God in Christ, and, if this is truly so, it can only affect our attitude and behaviour towards others. Belief and behaviour cannot be separated. The gospel has social consequences. It is a case of 'Freely you have received, freely give' (Matt. 10:8). 'And of His fullness we have all received, and grace for grace' (John 1:16). There is nothing 'stingy' or legalistic about the God of the Bible. 'He is kind to the unthankful and evil' (Luke 6:35).

In exhorting His followers to 'go the second mile', therefore, the Lord Jesus is exhorting all God's adopted children to act like their heavenly Father and guard the good name of His family, ensuring that we bear the family likeness of our generous Father above, reflecting something of the love and grace we have received from Him.

The Lord Jesus Christ Himself certainly 'went the second mile' – and beyond – for us. He left heaven for earth so that we might go at last to heaven. He became man so that we might become the children of God. He died the agonizing death of Calvary, with its physical and spiritual sufferings, to procure our eternal salvation. The grace of God in Christ has indeed been lavishly given to undeserving, ill-deserving sinners … Jesus went beyond the second mile to procure our salvation. How, then, can we who profess to be His followers not do likewise, even to those whom we do not naturally like or are drawn to help. Jesus went the second mile for us. This being so, having demonstrated to us His love and grace, He can command, inspire and empower us to emulate Him and go the second mile too. 'And whoever compels you to go one mile, go with him two' (Matt. 5:41).

43

Turn the other cheek

The world has some sayings which, while amusing, are actually contrary to the teaching of Scripture and should never be part of a Christian's outlook and ethos. Such sayings include: 'Don't get mad – get even.' 'Do unto others before they do unto you.' And, 'Make sure that you get your retaliation in first.'

The above sayings apart, the world also admires those who 'turn the other cheek'. They are not so concerned with how we act, but with how we react. Someone is nasty to us. We even suffer a gross injustice. But instead of being nasty back or vengefully seeking redress, we 'turn the other cheek'. That is, we overlook the offence when we have every right to be offended. We do not retaliate and attempt to 'get even'. 'Turning the other cheek' is all about having the spirit of forgiveness and not taking vengeance and seeking revenge on someone for the way they have spoken to us or treated us. Impossible? No. For there is such a phenomenon as the grace of God. 'With men it is impossible, but not with God; for with God all things are possible' (Mark 10:27).

The actual saying 'turn the other cheek' originates from an exhortation the Lord Jesus gave in His famous Sermon on the Mount. There, Jesus said, 'But I tell you not to resist an evil person. But whoever slaps you on your right cheek, turn the other to him also' (Matt. 5:39).

Consider the Saviour

The Saviour here was encouraging a spirit of non-retaliation and non-resistance in His followers' personal relationships. And Jesus certainly practised what He preached. Some years later,

Peter – one of the Saviour's closest followers – recalled how 'when He was reviled, [He] did not revile in return; when He suffered, He did not threaten, but committed Himself to Him who judges righteously' (1 Pet. 2:23).

In the first-century Graeco-Roman world of the Saviour's earthly ministry, when a victim was crucified, it was normal for that person to cry out in anguish and pain, and curse the cruel crucifiers. When the Lord Jesus was nailed to the cross of Calvary, however, instead of cursing the cruel perpetrators of His death, He prayed for those who crucified Him: 'Father, forgive them, for they do not know what they do' (Luke 23:34). The forgiveness of sins through the death of Christ on the cross lies at the very heart of the Christian gospel:

> *He died that we might be forgiven,*
> *He died to make us good,*
> *That we might go at last to heaven,*
> *Saved by His precious blood!*

> (MRS C. F. ALEXANDER, 1818–95)

Consider Stephen

It might be objected that Jesus is in a different category than His followers. He is the sinless Son of God. Is it the case, therefore, that He could 'turn the other cheek' but not so His followers? Was the Lord Jesus making an unreasonable demand? Evidently not. When Stephen, the first Christian martyr, was being stoned to death because of his love for Jesus, Luke records how he, too, prayed lovingly for the very people who threw the stones at him. 'He knelt down and cried out with a loud voice, "Lord, do not charge them with this sin." And when he had said this, he fell asleep' (Acts 7:60).

Consider Ourselves

Jesus, therefore, exhorts His followers in all the eras of time to be loving and forgiving. We have received the love and forgiveness of God. How incongruous, then, it is for us not to 'turn the other cheek' and display something of the love and forgiveness of God which we have received. 'And be kind to one another, tenderhearted, forgiving one another, even as God in Christ forgave you' (Eph. 4:32).

Some of us carry deep hurts from the hands of others. Jesus never said that 'turning the other cheek' would be a simple matter. What do we do when we have been a victim of injustice or cruelty? The first Christian reaction is to turn to God. 'Therefore let those who suffer according to the will of God commit their souls to Him in doing good, as to a faithful Creator' (1 Pet. 4:19). We have the privilege of both praying for ourselves and praying for our enemies. Our God is a God of both mercy and justice. Vengeance is not our prerogative – but it is His. In His infinite love, wisdom and justice, He has a way of righting wrongs. The vengeance of God is a truth of the Bible which is not popularly known or preached – but it is there. The matter of vengeance is much safer in God's hands than in ours, as He is infinite in justice and does not suffer from the wounded pride from which we suffer, tempting us to go 'over the top' in our desire to get even. Hence, Paul's exhortation to hand over the matter of vengeance to God: 'Beloved, never avenge yourselves, but leave it to the wrath of God, for it is written, "Vengeance is mine, I will repay, says the Lord"' (Rom. 12:19, ESV).

Therefore, as Christians, in obedience to our Saviour, we are to 'turn the other cheek' when we are hurt and wronged. By the grace of God, Christians are both different and called to act differently from the world. We are the adopted children of God, and as such inhabit a Christian counter-culture and obey the laws of heaven. Christians have a radically different world view and practice from the non-Christian world. We are loved by God, and, as such, are called to manifest that love – not just to our friends, but also to our enemies. In the light of God's grace and mercy, Jesus commands us to 'turn the other cheek'. In the light of God's love, Jesus tells us to 'Love your enemies, bless those who curse you, do good to those who hate you, and pray for those who spitefully use you and persecute you, that you may be sons of your Father in heaven …' (Matt. 5:44, 45).

44

From strength to strength

Two everyday expressions in popular use are at opposite ends of the spectrum. One goes, 'He's gone from bad to worse.' The other goes, 'He's gone from strength to strength.' This chapter is concerned with the latter expression. If we say to someone, 'May you go from strength to strength', we mean something like, 'May you have increasing success.' Thus a best man at a wedding, when he toasts the bride and groom, might say, 'We all hope and pray that your marriage will go from strength to strength.' The marriage began happily with love, so the wish is that the couple's love for each other will grow further and fuller in the days ahead. Then there is the example of a champion boxer. They say that nothing succeeds like success. He has won the British title. After a successful defence of this, he progresses to the European title, and even has designs on a world-title shot. He gains in confidence and experience with each title defence. He goes 'from strength to strength'.

It may surprise you to know that the expression 'from strength to strength' is taken from Psalm 84:7. There we read: 'They go from strength to strength; every one of them appears before God in Zion.' Psalm 84 is a psalm of delight in the temple of God and the God of the temple. Paradoxically, the omnipresent God of the universe made Himself present in a special, particular and localized way in the temple at Jerusalem – and the Psalmist was travelling to Jerusalem to meet God there. He just could not contain his longing and delight. 'How lovely is Your tabernacle, O LORD of hosts! My soul longs, yes, even faints for the courts of the LORD; my heart and my flesh cry out for the living God' (Ps. 84:1, 2).

'For a day in Your courts is better than a thousand ... (v. 10). 'For the LORD God is a sun and shield; the LORD will give grace and glory'... (v. 11).

When travelling to Jerusalem, however, the Psalmist faced certain difficulties and trials – as indeed do all Christians as they travel to the heavenly Jerusalem. The Psalmist and his companions had to 'pass through the Valley of Baca' (Ps. 84:6). This could refer to a dry, barren, desolate place, or it could be metaphorical, for literally it means 'the valley of weeping'. The difficulties and discouragements apart, however, the Psalmist kept travelling. His anticipation of meeting with the living God at his journey's end kept him going forward. It was a case of 'the joy of the LORD is your strength' (Neh. 8:10). He knew the strength, sustenance and refreshment which only God can give. Hence, he could testify: 'Blessed is the man whose strength is in You, whose heart is set on pilgrimage. As they pass through the Valley of Baca, they make it a spring; the rain also covers it with pools. *They go from strength to strength*; every one of them appears before God in Zion' (Ps. 84:5-7, emphasis mine).

And so the Psalmist 'went from strength to strength'. He was happy in the Lord, who is the fount of every blessing. And his current happiness would only get greater when he actually arrived in the temple of God and drew nearer to the God of the temple, who is the God of the whole universe. 'They go from strength to strength.' This is true; and this is to be true in relation to the Christian life, in both its earthly and eternal facets.

Earthly Facets

There is to be a progression in the Christian life. Pilgrims should make progress. When we are first saved by God's grace, we are made aware of His great love for us. We are then to grow in our love for and service of God for all our remaining earthly days – going 'from strength to strength'. Peter closes his second letter with the exhortation 'Grow in the grace and knowledge of our Lord and Savior Jesus Christ' (2 Pet. 3:18). There is no short cut to Christian maturity. Yet we cannot progress in the Christian faith unless we utilize the means of grace God has given us – daily prayer, daily and consecutive reading of the Bible, attendance at public worship to hear God's Word explained and applied, and the fellowship and encouragement of other Christians travelling the same pilgrim pathway. It is also the universal testimony of Christians that 'there is no gain without pain'. God, in His providence, will send trials and suffering our way. These are the means by which we will grow. He will prune His vine so that it will bear fruit. Trials cast us more closely on God for help and strength and wean us away from the temporal things of earth. They also teach us lessons in human sympathy – and in doing so, they make us more like Him who is infinite in sympathy, our Lord and Saviour Jesus Christ.

Eternal Facets

The Christian life is to go from strength to strength, and the Christian life will surely yet go from strength to strength. We are marching to Zion, the beautiful city of God! By God's grace we will reach the heavenly Jerusalem. The best is yet to be. 'His servants shall serve Him. They shall see His face …' (Rev. 22:3, 4). We know something of the joy of God's salvation now – but the joy of our present salvation will only increase. Grace is glory begun. But glory will be grace consummated. The joy of glory will be – according to the Bible – like an eternal wedding feast. Our salvation will then be complete, and our joy will know no bounds. 'Let us be glad and rejoice and give Him glory, for the marriage of the Lamb has come … Blessed are those who are called to the marriage supper of the Lamb' (Rev. 19:7, 9).

The Christian life, therefore – a life saved, sanctified, strengthened and consummated by God's grace – is truly a life that goes 'from strength to strength'. It does so because the eternal purposes of God are invincible. He cannot be thwarted from fulfilling His eternal covenant of grace to give eternal blessing to His people to the eternal glory of His name. 'The path of the just is like the shining sun, that shines ever brighter unto the perfect day' (Prov. 4:18).

45

A heart of stone

We normally use the description 'a heart of stone' in a somewhat derogatory way. It describes someone who is unfeeling, callous and even inhuman. If a person is considered to have no sympathy at all towards the plight of another, 'It's as if he has a heart of stone' – that is, he is inwardly unmoved by the suffering of a fellow human being, possesses no desire to help, and is unconcerned, even 'dead' to that person's predicament.

The expression 'a heart of stone' is actually a biblical one. In Ezekiel 36:26, God Himself promises, 'I will give you a new heart and put a new spirit within you; I will take *the heart of stone* out of your flesh and give you a heart of flesh' (emphasis added). From this, we glean that salvation entails a spiritual heart transplant, and the surgeon who performs this operation is none less than Almighty God Himself.

Heart trouble

The Bible's diagnosis of us is that, spiritually speaking, we are all born with 'hearts of stone', that is, we are born spiritually dead – dead to God, dead to our spiritual condition as sinners, and dead to eternity. The heart of the problem is the problem of the heart.

As we have already seen, in the Bible the 'heart' refers not so much to the physical organ which pumps the blood, but to the inner being – the soul, the seat of our emotions, affections and desires. When the Bible diagnoses us with 'hearts of stone', therefore, it is saying that, by nature, we are less than fully alive. Sin has deadened us to God, the fount of every blessing. Dead people cannot respond to God's voice, no matter how loudly the gospel is preached to them. Salvation thus entails being made spiritually alive. And this God does, by His Holy Spirit. The technical term for this is 'regeneration' – a spiritual rebirth. 'And you He made alive, who were dead in trespasses and sins, in which you once walked ...' (Eph. 2:1, 2). 'But God, who is rich in mercy, because of His great love with which He loved us, even when we were dead in trespasses, made us alive together with Christ (by grace you have been saved)' (Eph. 2:4, 5).

A Heart Transplant

To put this another way, salvation entails a heart transplant. Salvation involves the divine removal of the heart of stone responsible for our spiritual deadness, and the implantation of a heart of flesh in its place – a heart that thinks and pulsates spiritually; a heart that responds to the grace of God. God's promise is this: 'I will take the heart of stone out of your flesh and give you a heart of flesh.' In His mercy, God enables us – He 'gives us a heart' – to respond to Him. By the regenerating power of His Holy Spirit, He raises us to new, spiritual life. He makes us aware of His existence. He convicts us of our sin and lost plight – that we are not right with Him. He then shows us His Son, the crucified Saviour, and He draws us to the foot of the cross and enables us to put our faith in Him and receive Him as our own, personal Saviour. We are now reconciled to God. We are now fully alive! Our hearts of stone have been removed. We are now alive to God and motivated to know, love and serve Him in response to His love. Salvation entails our hearts of stone being replaced by a heart of flesh. It is all God's doing. Salvation is wholly and solely 'of the Lord'. It is so because hearts of stone are incapable of exercising saving faith. Dead people cannot believe in Jesus. Saving faith is the consequence, not the cause of divine regeneration.

A heart of stone

So, thank God that salvation is both divinely accomplished and divinely applied. It was accomplished by God in Christ at Calvary. It is applied by God through the agency of His Holy Spirit to human souls – applied to hearts of stone, giving them new and eternal life in Christ, enabling them to respond to the grace of God. The Holy Spirit's indispensable role in our salvation must not be overlooked. He is indispensable because by nature we have 'hearts of stone'. And only the regenerating and renewing power of God can change a heart of stone. *The Westminster Shorter Catechism* states:

> *We are made partakers of the redemption purchased by Christ by the effectual application of it to us by His Holy Spirit.*

> *The Spirit applieth to us the redemption purchased by Christ by working faith in us, and thereby uniting us to Christ in our effectual calling.*

> *Effectual calling is the work of God's Spirit whereby, con-vincing us of our sin and misery, enlightening our minds in the knowledge of Christ, and renewing our wills, He doth persuade and enable us to embrace Jesus Christ, freely offered to us in the Gospel.*[1]

---

1. *The Westminster Shorter Catechism,* Questions 29, 30, 31

46

Judas!

Hopefully, we will never accuse someone of being a 'Judas'. The word is used to accuse, insult and abuse. During the U.K. miners' strike of 1984, those who crossed the picket line had various insults hurled at them. Among these were the words 'Scab!' and 'Judas!'

The name 'Judas' is infamous. Why? Because it was Judas Iscariot, one of Jesus' twelve chosen disciples, who was responsible for betraying the Lord Jesus. Judas's betrayal subsequently led to Christ's being arrested by the Jewish authorities and handed over to the Roman authorities, who put Him to death by crucifixion. The name 'Judas' is thus synonymous with treachery and betrayal. The words 'Judas' and 'traitor' are interchangeable.

Judas's exact motives for doing what he did are debated. One of them, however, was monetary gain. 'One of the twelve, called Judas Iscariot, went to the chief priests and said, "What are you willing to give me if I deliver Him to you?" And they counted out to him thirty pieces of silver' (Matt. 26:14, 15).

No new parents in their right mind would name their baby 'Judas'. Judas is one of the most infamous figures of history. But are there any lessons to be gleaned from this notorious man? Yes, there are.

The Divine Scriptures

Judas's betrayal of the Lord Jesus did not take Him by surprise, for both he and his action had been predicted centuries beforehand in the Holy Scriptures. Psalm 41:9 is prophetic when it reads 'Even my own familiar friend in whom I trusted, who ate my bread, has lifted up his heel against me.' That this refers ultimately to Judas at the 'Last Supper' is patent from the New Testament, when 'the Lord Jesus on the same night in which He was betrayed took bread' (1 Cor. 11:23).

The atmosphere in the Upper Room chilled when Jesus announced that one of the twelve disciples would betray Him. The disciples, understandably, wondered who it would be and who it could be. 'Jesus answered, "It is he to whom I shall give a piece of bread when I have dipped it." And having dipped the bread, He gave it to Judas Iscariot, the son of Simon' (John 13:26). Judas then left the supper table, and betrayed Jesus to the authorities. Jesus had already explained, 'I know whom I have chosen; but that the Scripture may be fulfilled, "He who eats bread with Me has lifted up his heel against Me"' (John 13:18). The Scripture was now fulfilled. 'The Son of Man indeed goes just as it is written of Him, but woe to that man by whom the Son of Man is betrayed!' (Matt. 26:24).

The fulfilment of Scripture is one of the many evidences that the Bible is the Word of God. Only the eternal God knows the end from the beginning, hence only He can reveal history in advance.

The Divine Sympathy

The Lord Jesus was betrayed, not by an enemy, but by a friend, 'my own familiar friend in whom I trusted'. Jesus chose twelve disciples, and Judas was one of these. Thus Judas, along with the eleven, lived closely with Jesus for the three years of His ministry. He imbibed His teaching. He witnessed His miracles. They ate at the same table, slept under the same roof, travelled together, attended weddings and funerals together, and worshipped in the synagogue together. Finally ... Judas betrayed his Master.

We recall that Jesus was and is as fully human as divine. His humanity was real. He felt pain – psychological as well as physical. Psychologically, the betrayal by a supposed friend is more hurtful than the hostility of an enemy. The latter is to be expected; the former is not. From all this, we can say that our God is no remote deity. He knows what it is like to be human. In Christ, He shared our human lot. Jesus is thus a Saviour of infinite sympathy. 'Jesus wept' (John 11:35). 'For we do not have a High Priest who cannot sympathize with our weaknesses, but was in all points tempted as we are, yet without sin' (Heb. 4:15).

> *With joy we meditate the grace*
> *Of our High Priest above;*
> *His heart is made of tenderness*
> *And overflows with love.*
>
> *Touched with a sympathy within,*
> *He knows our feeble frame;*
> *He knows what sore temptation means*
> *For He has felt the same.*

(ISAAC WATTS, 1674–1748)

The Divine Sovereignty

Judas's betrayal of the Lord Jesus has gone down in history as one of the most wicked acts of all time. His act led to the crucifixion of the very Son of God. Yet, paradoxically, the evil intentions of sinful men were, unfathomably, also an act of God, and the supreme demonstration of His grace to sinners. For the death of Jesus has procured the greatest blessing of all – it has procured the eternal salvation of all who put their trust in Him. Contradictory though it may appear, man's worst deed actually wrought God's best work.

We are dealing here with a deep mystery beyond our human comprehension – the mystery of the relation between human responsibility and divine sovereignty. Judas was fully responsible for his betrayal. He did what he did willingly – yet it was all foreordained by God. Likewise, those who nailed the Saviour to the cross were fully responsible and accountable for their action – but ultimately, it was God the Father, not they, who put His Son to death. 'He … did not spare His own Son, but delivered Him up for us all' (Rom. 8:32). 'He loved us and sent His Son to be the propitiation for our sins' (1 John 4:10). The death of Christ on the cross was ultimately an act of God, integral to His eternal plan of salvation to save a people for Himself and His glory. And what God foreordained in eternity past, He brought about in time and space – even using sinful men like Judas to accomplish His eternal purposes of grace. Judas's betrayal of Jesus was wicked – yet it was a link in the golden chain of divine salvation. Humanly speaking, the salvation of the cross would not have been wrought had he not played his part.

On the Day of Pentecost, Peter explained: 'Him [that is, Jesus] being delivered by the determined purpose and foreknowledge of God, you have taken by lawless hands, have crucified, and put to death' (Acts 2:23). Such are the wonders of God's providence and redemption. Our God reigns! He will have His way. His will will most certainly be done.

> *Deep in unfathomable mines*
> *Of never-failing skill,*
> *He treasures up His bright designs,*
> *And works His sovereign will.*

(WILLIAM COWPER, 1731–1800)

'Judas!' It is a distasteful expression to use. But Judas Iscariot, one of the infamous characters of history, actually encourages us. He draws our attention to the divine inspiration of the Holy Scriptures. He reminds us of the divine sympathy of our Saviour. And he reinforces to us the total and absolute sovereignty of our God over all things – the only true comfort to our souls.

47

The twinkling of an eye

If something happens 'in the twinkling of an eye', it happens in an instant. It happens in a flash – a microsecond. The synonym for 'the twinkling of an eye' is 'the blink of an eye'. The eye is a very sensitive organ. Blinking is necessary to protect it from irritation. Blinking also provides moisture to the eye through the irrigation provided by the tear ducts, and so lubricates the eye with the lubricant that the eyes secrete. A blink is a very quick, involuntary action. A blink takes just 300-400 milliseconds to complete.

The saying 'In the twinkling of an eye' originates in 1 Corinthians 15 in the New Testament. First Corinthians 15 is the famous 'Resurrection Chapter' of the Bible. In it, the Apostle Paul draws our attention to both the historical reality of the resurrection of Christ from the dead and the consequent bodily resurrection at the Last Day of all who are united to Christ in saving faith. According to the Apostle, the final resurrection and consummation of all things will be one, climactic event. He explains: 'Behold, I tell you a mystery: we shall not all sleep, but we shall all be changed – in a moment, *in the twinkling of an eye*, at the last trumpet. For the trumpet will sound, and the dead will be raised incorruptible, and we shall be changed' (1 Cor. 15:51, 52, emphasis added).

The Resurrection of the Body

The ultimate and final Christian 'hope' – by which the Bible means a confident expectation and anticipation, based on the promises of God – is not so much the salvation of the soul, but the resurrection of the body. This, the Bible says, will occur at the Second Coming of Christ at the end of the age. 'We also eagerly wait for the Saviour, the Lord Jesus Christ, who will transform our lowly body that it may be conformed to His glorious body, according to the working by which He is able even to subdue all things to Himself' (Phil. 3:20, 21).

Christians have already experienced a spiritual resurrection. This is known in the Bible as regeneration or the new and second birth. 'And you He made alive, who were dead in trespasses and sins, in which you once walked ...' (Eph. 2:1, 2). 'But God, who is rich in mercy, because of His great love with which He loved us, even when we were dead in trespasses, made us alive together with Christ (by grace you have been saved)' (Eph. 2:4, 5). Yet this spiritual resurrection – our current salvation – is enjoyed and experienced in a body which is less than perfect, as in this age even the fittest of us is subject to varying degrees of physical and mental pain, handicap, illness, etc., and will eventually die. A basic, but sometimes neglected, fundamental of the Christian faith, however, is recorded in the Apostles' Creed: 'I believe ... in the resurrection of the body, and the life everlasting, Amen.' The Bible holds out the prospect of the redemption of the body as well as the soul. This will be the Christian's full and final salvation – its ultimate consummation. Christians are promised new bodies, suitable for serving God in a new heaven and a new earth, 'because the creation itself also will be delivered from the bondage of corruption into the glorious liberty of the children of God ... And not only that, but we also who have the firstfruits of the Spirit, even we ourselves groan within ourselves, eagerly waiting for the adoption, the redemption of our body' (Rom. 8:21, 23). Here is the most thrilling prospect of all!

But what exactly will the Christian's resurrection body be like? Greater than we can describe! But it will be like Christ's resurrection body, for 'Christ is risen from the dead, and has become the firstfruits of those who have fallen asleep' (1 Cor. 15:20). Our resurrection bodies will thus, paradoxically, be 'similar but different'. The risen Christ was recognizable as Jesus of Nazareth – yet the risen Christ could also appear and disappear at will and walk through solid walls. The resurrection body will thus not be subject to its current frustrations and limitations. Above all, it will be a suitable vehicle for serving God for all eternity, free from our present hindrances and handicaps.

By analogy …

In 1 Corinthians 15, Paul likens the relationship between the Christian's present and future body to the relationship between a seed and a flower. One day, we will be buried in the grave. But at the last day, we will flourish and blossom as never before. Our bodies now will perish – but then they will be imperishable. Our bodies now are mortal – but then they will be immortal. Our bodies now are weak – then they will be strong. Our bodies now are, as it were, in a state of humiliation – then they will be glorified. Our bodies now are suitable for living on earth – then they will be animated by God's Holy Spirit, suitable for living in the eternal kingdom of God. Our bodies now are similar to the first, sinful Adam's. Our bodies then will be like the last Adam's – like the body of the risen, glorified Lord Jesus Christ.

The Resurrection Faith

The Christian faith is a resurrection faith. At its heart lies an empty tomb and a risen Saviour. The coming resurrection of all believers is a consequence of Christ's redeeming work and a consequence of His resurrection. The Bible says that it will really happen. When? In God's time, at the Last Day. How? Very quickly – 'in the twinkling of an eye' – 'in a moment, in the twinkling of an eye, at the last trumpet. For the trumpet will sound, and the dead will be raised incorruptible, and we shall be changed' (1 Cor. 15:52).

48

Fight the good fight!

'Fight the good fight!' This expression is popularly used as an exhortation – an encouragement to persevere and press on in spite of the difficulties and discouragements. Picture a scene in winter. It is a cold, Monday morning. The alarm wakes you up. Your instinct is to pull the duvet over you and stay in bed. But you have to go to work. Eventually, you are found standing on a railway platform, shivering in the cold, waiting for the 07.50 to arrive. A work colleague joins you. 'Fight the good fight,' he says, with a sheepish grin.

The exhortation to 'fight the good fight' originates from a personal letter of the Apostle Paul to Timothy, a young pastor. It is found in 1 Timothy 6:12, but with an important addition to its popular use. 1 Timothy 6:12 is specific when it states, 'Fight the good fight *of faith*' (emphasis mine). The original expression is thus specifically Christian. And the original expression is closely in line with much of what Paul wrote in his pastoral letter to Timothy, whom he describes as 'my true son in the faith' (1 Tim. 1:2). Paul was fond of using military metaphors. Paul's exhortation no doubt put iron in Timothy's spine, just when he needed it.

Timothy

Timothy – the recipient of our expression – was based in Ephesus. He was a gifted church leader, yet he was prone to discouragement, timidity and bouts of ill health. Paul thus wrote to Timothy to encourage him. He wrote that he might 'be a good minister of Jesus Christ' (1 Tim. 4:6); that he might 'be an example to the believers in word, in conduct, in love, in spirit, in faith , in purity'

(1 Tim. 4:12); that as he led and fed his congregation he 'might know how you ought to conduct yourself in the house of God, which is the church of the living God, the pillar and ground of the truth' (1 Tim. 3:15).

As Timothy was a leader in the church militant on earth, he was at the forefront of the battle for the gospel. He faced difficulties on the outside and discouragement within. This being so, Paul brought his letter to a rousing close with words to the effect of the hymn 'Onward Christian soldiers, marching as to war ...' 'Fight the good fight of faith,' Paul urged.

'Fight the good fight of faith.' The exhortation is a timely one to all members of the church militant on earth. Ease is for heaven, but not for earth. From the moment of our salvation, we are engaged in a spiritual battle against the world, the flesh and the devil. As Warren Wiersbe has said, 'The Christian life is a battleground, not a playground.' The hymn writer exhorts us:

> *Stand up, stand up for Jesus!*
> *The strife will not be long.*
> *This day the noise of battle,*
> *The next the victor's song!*

(GEORGE DUFFIELD, 1818–88)

Every Christian has enrolled in the army of King Jesus. We are thus obliged to 'fight the good fight of faith'. But what exactly does this mean in practice?

Fighting the good fight

In Jude 3, Jude writes, 'exhorting you to contend earnestly for the faith which was once for all delivered to the saints ...' The thought echoes our expression here in 1 Timothy 6:12. The original Greek verb which the Holy Spirit employs is '*agonizoo*', which we could translate and paraphrase as 'Continue to fight and struggle. Continue to strive and contend perseveringly against all opposition and temptation.' 'Carry on the struggle.' Literally, 1 Timothy 6:12 may be rendered as 'Keep on fighting the good fight (the word is '*agon*') of *the faith*.' 'The faith' is a reference to the Christian faith – the revealed truth of God as it is in Jesus, preached by the apostles and inscripturated in God's written Word. So, in a nutshell, Paul is exhorting both Timothy and us to contend for Christian belief and behaviour; for Christian doctrine and Christian moral duty; for Christian truth and for a Christian lifestyle. It goes without saying, of course, that we should contend without being contentious – we should contend in the spirit of Christ – in a way that honours the Saviour, reflects the love of God and commends the gospel which has saved us.

1. Christians contend for Christian truth

False teachers abounded in Paul and Timothy's day, just as false doctrine is propagated today. Paul commenced his letter to Timothy urging him to 'remain in Ephesus that you may charge some that they teach no other doctrine' (1 Tim. 1:3).

While Christians may disagree on secondary issues, they are united in core belief – united in the fundamentals of the faith for which they contend. What are these fundamentals? They include the fact that there is but one true and living God who created the universe, and this God exists – and has existed eternally – in the three Persons of the Father, Son and Holy Spirit. They include the fact of the Lord Jesus Christ – His absolute deity and His real humanity. They include the fact of the Fall – that we are sinners who need to be saved and the fact that Jesus is the only Saviour of sinners. They include the fact of Christ's virgin birth, sinless life and the miracles He performed to confirm His divine identity. They major on the fact of His atoning death in the place of sinners and His conquest of the grave three days later. They include the fact that He will come again in power and great glory. They include the fact of the necessity of saving faith in Jesus, and the realities of both an eternal heaven and an eternal hell. Christians thus 'fight the good fight of faith' – they contend for the faith of the Bible; they contend for the saving truth of the Bible – the non-negotiable fundamentals necessary for our eternal salvation.

2. Christians contend for Christian living

We live in an age of 'laissez-faire' – anything goes. Christians, however, are adamant that the Bible contains our Maker's instructions. The sovereign God has every right to tell us how to behave. God our Maker knows what the best way is for us to live for our true well-being. Christians thus seek to obey God's commandments. We have a moral obligation to obey God's moral law, as well as an obligation to abhor anything which is contrary to it. Is this a 'tall order'? Yes, it is, but thank God that He gives us His Holy Spirit. He grants us the power to live in the way He would have us live. 'His commandments are not burdensome' (1 John 5:3). Christians thus contend against anything contrary to the Word of God in their personal, social, ecclesiastical and national life. A Christian loves what God loves, obeys what God commands, hates what God hates, and prohibits what God prohibits, knowing that God knows best. A Christian 'fights the good fight of the faith'.

The Christian life, then, really is a battleground and not a playground. In the life to come, we will lay down our sword and shield – but not in this life. There are many adversaries, but by God's grace we continue to 'fight the good faith of faith' – contending for Christian doctrine and duty. Glorious ease will be our experience in heaven. This life, though, is characterized by a continual fight against the sin within and the evil in the world and all that is opposed to Christ and His cause. But we would have it no other way. If we belong to Jesus, we are on the winning side! God has no losers and the devil has no winners. 'Thanks be to God, who gives us the victory through our Lord Jesus Christ' (1 Cor. 15:57). So, 'Fight the good fight!'

> *Fight the good fight with all thy might;*
> *Christ is thy strength and Christ thy right.*
> *Lay hold on life and it shall be*
> *Thy joy and crown eternally!*
>
> *Faint not nor fear, His arms are near,*
> *He changeth not, and thou art dear.*
> *Only believe, and thou shalt see*
> *That Christ is all in all to thee!*

(JOHN SAMUEL BEWLEY MONSELL, 1811–75)

49

You reap what you sow

Popular wisdom generally agrees that 'we reap what we sow'. That is, certain consequences inexorably follow certain actions, just as a grain of wheat when sown produces wheat and not a sunflower. Thus, a person who is addicted to smoking will eventually pay the price for such a habit with lung cancer. A person who overeats and under-exercises will suffer from obesity and the health problems it brings. A person who is persistently late for work, and ignores the warnings against this, will eventually lose his job. Reaping what we sow, therefore, refers to what is also known as 'cause and effect'.

The metaphorical 'reaping what we sow', however, does not always follow on strictly. Most people have come across smokers who justify their habit by saying, 'My granny lived until she was ninety-seven, and she smoked like a chimney.' Then there are those who break the rules at work and yet always seem to get away with it without being punished. And there are also those who are diligent at work, and work hard, yet never get promotion. Also, there are those who follow all the supposed 'rules' which promote good health, yet are still struck down by terminal illness.

The apparent discrepancies and injustices of life perplexed the writers of the Bible as much as they perplex us. In Ecclesiastes 8:14, for instance, we read, 'There is a vanity that takes place on earth, that there are righteous people to whom it happens according to the deeds of the wicked, and there are wicked people to whom it happens according to the deeds of the righteous. I said that this also is vanity' (ESV). Psalm 73 is also taken up with the Psalmist's vexation at observing the wicked prospering and the righteous suffering. And in the Book of Job we read how a godly, God-fearing man nevertheless suffered all kinds of losses, trials, suffering and pain.

The Expression

The expression 'You reap what you sow' is a biblical one. Its use in the Bible concerns the inevitable eternal consequences, rather than uncertain earthly consequences, of what we do or do not do. The text in question is found in Galatians 6:7, 8, where we read the warning: 'Do not be deceived, God is not mocked; for whatever a man sows, that he will also reap. For he who sows to his flesh will of the flesh reap corruption, but he who sows to the Spirit will of the Spirit reap everlasting life.' What is Paul teaching here? The *New Bible Commentary* explains:

> *The general principle is clearly that unreceptiveness to gospel teaching and indulgence in casual pursuits will bear its own fruit. What a man sows he will reap. From fleshly indulgence issues decay leading to destruction. On the contrary, to sow 'to the Spirit' means devoting the energies of life to the values of the Spirit of God revealed in and by Jesus Christ. That which is of the Spirit yields life eternal. A man deceives only himself when he supposes that he can turn up his nose at God with impunity. No one can hoodwink God.'* [1]

Eternal Consequences

This eternal facet of 'sowing and reaping', then, is a warning to the non-Christian. This world is not the be-all and end-all. There is more to life than eating, drinking, working, marrying and enjoying the legitimate and illegitimate thrills of time and space. This world will pass away. By nature, we are – to quote Jonathan Edwards

---

1. Samuel J. Mikolaski in the Galatians chapter of the *New Bible Commentary Revised,* Third Edition, ed. D. Guthrie, J. A. Motyer, A. M. Stibbs and D. J. Wiseman, InterVarsity Press, (Leicester, 1970), p. 1104.

– 'Sinners in the hands of an angry God.' Our greatest need is for a Saviour. Our attitude towards the Saviour in time determines where we will spend eternity. 'He who believes in the Son has everlasting life; and he who does not believe the Son shall not see life, but the wrath of God abides on him' (John 3:36).The cross of Christ is the only roadblock to hell that there is. Hence the vital necessity of trusting Him now, lest we reap the eternal consequences of eternal destruction. 'Behold, now is the accepted time; behold, now is the day of salvation' (2 Cor. 6:2).

The eternal facet of 'sowing and reaping', however, also has an application to the Christian. 'The things which are seen are temporary, but the things which are not seen are eternal' (2 Cor. 4:18). It was to Christians that John was writing when he warned that 'all that is in the world – the lust of the flesh, the lust of the eyes, and the pride of life – is not of the Father but is of the world. And the world is passing away, and the lust of it; but he who does the will of God abides forever' (1 John 2:16, 17). This being so, we should ask ourselves whether we are investing our time, energy and resources for time or for eternity. Is our main preoccupation the eternal matters of God or the passing things of time? Do we employ our time and money to 'sow to the Spirit' – propagating the gospel and growing in the faith – or are we mainly concerned with pursuits which, although legitimate, will pass away and have no eternal consequences? 'Only one life, 'twill soon be past, only what's done for Christ will last.'[2] The good can detract us from the best. The temporal can detract us from the eternal. The things of the world can impede our enjoyment of, in John Newton's famous words, the 'solid joys and lasting treasure' which 'none but Zion's children know'.

---

2. A saying popularized by C.T. Studd

The question is: What really absorbs my heart and mind day by day? Paul exhorts, 'If then you were raised with Christ, seek those things which are above, where Christ is, sitting at the right hand of God. Set your mind on things above, not on things on the earth' (Col. 3:1, 2).

Do we reap what we sow? The answer, in this life, is 'Often, but not always.' The answer in the light of eternity, though, is 'Most certainly.' Why? 'Do not be deceived, God is not mocked; for *whatever a man sows, that he will also reap.* For he who sows to the flesh will of the flesh reap corruption, but he who sows to the Spirit will of the Spirit reap everlasting life' (Gal. 6:7, 8, emphasis mine).

50
Crystal clear

'The instructions on the package were crystal clear,' said the man, proudly, after he had assembled a bookcase from a flat pack. We use the description 'crystal clear' to refer to something that is understood. A teacher, having explained a concept, might check the comprehension of the class by asking, 'Is this all clear to you'?

The description 'clear as crystal' comes from the last two chapters of the last Book of the Bible – the Book of Revelation. It is used there to capture something of the glorious existence which awaits God's redeemed people in the age to come. John the Apostle, the author of Revelation, was given a vision of the redeemed universe which God will inaugurate in His good time. 'And I saw a new heaven and a new earth, for the first heaven and the first earth had passed away …' (Rev. 21:1). This redeemed universe is likened to both a garden city and a bride of indescribable beauty and excellence: 'the holy city, New Jerusalem, coming down out of heaven from God, prepared as a bride adorned for her husband' (Rev. 21:2). The glory of this city just cannot be put into words, for its glory is the reflected glory of God Himself. John thus describes it – under the inspiration of the Holy Spirit – by using the analogies of the best and most precious and exquisite things of earth: its 'having the glory of God. Her light was like a most precious stone, like a jasper stone, *clear as crystal'* (Rev. 21:11, emphasis mine). Then, among the many awesome wonders of this city, John records that it contains 'a pure river of water of life, *clear as crystal*, proceeding from the throne of God and of the Lamb' (Rev. 22:1, emphasis mine).

The language of Revelation is highly symbolic. The question is, though: Symbolic of what? What do the glorious, crystal-clear waters which proceed from both the Father and the Son in glory mean?

Edenic Restoration

At the dawn of time, we note that the Garden of Eden enjoyed the benefits of a river. Genesis 2:10 tells us: 'Now a river went out of Eden to water the garden, and from there it parted and became four riverheads.' When we read the last two chapters of the Bible, we cannot help noticing the resemblances and echoes there of the Garden of Eden – Paradise – before sin came in and spoiled things. Both Eden and the eternal kingdom of heaven possess an unpolluted river; both Eden and glory have the tree of life in their midst; and both Eden and the new heavens and the new earth are characterized by unblemished fellowship with God for their occupants. We read in Revelation 22:3, 4, that in the age to come 'There shall be no more curse, but the throne of God and of the Lamb shall be in it, and His servants shall serve Him. They shall see His face, and His name shall be on their foreheads.'

The Bible, therefore, is a Book which comes to a full circle. It begins in a garden and it ends in a garden. It begins with a river and it ends with a river. The main themes of the Bible are Creation, the Fall and Redemption – Paradise Lost and Paradise Restored. The redemption procured by God in Christ is both a present redemption and a promised redemption. It will reach its consummation in a new heaven and a new earth. 'The creation itself also will be delivered from the bondage of corruption into the glorious liberty of the children of God' (Rom. 8:21). The redeemed of Christ will one day inhabit redeemed bodies in a redeemed universe. It will be akin to Eden before the Fall, when

Adam and Eve enjoyed unhindered and unblemished fellowship with God their Maker. Yet it will be even greater than that, for standing this side of Calvary and the empty tomb means that God's people now know even more of the grace and love of God than Adam knew in Eden:

> *Where He displays His healing power,*
> *Death and the curse are known no more.*
> *In Him the tribes of Adam boast*
> *More blessings than their father lost!*

> (ISAAC WATTS, 1674–1748)

Full Salvation

Pure, clean water is essential for life and health – for drinking and cleanliness. Many of the major cities of the world were built by a river. The water from the river was vital for both the health of the population and for industry. The crystal-clear waters of glory thus speak to us about the life, refreshment, joy and satisfaction which will be enjoyed by all its blessed inhabitants. 'You give them drink from the river of Your pleasures. For with You is the fountain of life' (Ps. 36:8, 9). 'There is a river whose streams shall make glad the city of God, the holy place of the tabernacle of the Most High' (Ps. 46:4).

Notice that the blessed river in glory is described as 'proceeding from the throne of God and of the Lamb' (Rev. 22:1) – that is, it flows from the Father and the Son. This suggests that the river in glory refers to the Holy Spirit of God, who is described by Jesus as 'the Helper, the Holy Spirit, whom the Father will send in My name' (John 14:26). The blessing of God always comes to us from God the Father, through the Son, by His Holy Spirit. Blessing is always triune.

The *Nicene Creed* states: 'I believe in the Holy Ghost, the Lord, the giver of life, who proceedeth from the Father and the Son.' The glorious, clear waters of the river of glory proceed from the Father and the Son. The glorious, clear waters of the river of glory remind us that, in the age to come, God's people will know and enjoy eternal life in a way they have never known before. It will be a life in all its fullness. It will entail enjoying the fullness of God's Holy Spirit – He who imparts the salvation of Christ and the blessing of God to us here on earth. The age to come, there-fore, will be an age of full salvation and full satisfaction. The Lord Jesus Himself once likened the life and blessing which the Holy Spirit imparts to the believer as being akin to a river of satisfaction within. He once gave the invitation: 'If anyone thirsts, let him come to Me and drink. He who believes in Me, as the Scripture has said, out of his heart will flow rivers of living water' (John 7:37, 38). John gave an editorial explanation of Jesus' words here: 'This He spoke concerning the Spirit, whom those believing in Him would receive …' (John 7:39).

Crystal Clear

The crystal-clear waters of glory, therefore, refer to life in all its fullness – full salvation and full satisfaction, by God, in God, free from all that hinders and handicaps our fellowship with Him in this present age. In glory, our needs will be fully, freely, finally and for ever met, by God the Father, through His Son, by His Holy Spirit. The crystal-clear river of His saving grace and satisfac-tion will never cease to flow – to our eternal blessing and God's eternal praise.

51
Make hay while the sun shines

'Make hay while the sun shines.' The expression has its origin in the farming community. We could paraphrase it like this: 'If the sun is shining, and the grass is ready to be cut, get out and cut it straight away. It might be raining tomorrow and scything in such conditions won't be so pleasant.'

The expression is also heard outside an agricultural, farming setting. It means something like this: 'Take your opportunity when it arises. You may not get another.' 'Don't put off until tomorrow what you can do today, as you might not get the opportunity tomorrow.' The author well remembers reading about a minister who was diagnosed with terminal cancer. Cancer concentrates the mind. The sufferer related how he enjoyed bonfire night on November 5, aware that he would never enjoy colourful fireworks on Guy Fawkes Night again. The same went for his Christmas celebrations with his family. It also affected his work and wider relations. He made the most of every opportunity, and kept 'short accounts' with both God and his friends, knowing that he did not have many days left on earth.

We will look in the Bible in vain to find the exact expression, 'Make hay while the sun shines.' But, that being said, the spirit and ethos of the saying is definitely scriptural. It has an application to both the non-Christian and to the Christian.

The Non-Christian

The Bible is permeated with urgent, evangelistic imperatives. Salvation is an urgent matter to be settled now – while the sun shines. Procrastination is both deadly and damnable, as we are not guaranteed the opportunity and ability to believe in Jesus in the unknown future. Hence Isaiah, the 'evangelical prophet', wrote: 'Seek the LORD while He may be found, call upon Him while He is near. Let the wicked forsake his way, and the unrighteous man his thoughts; let him return to the LORD, and He will have mercy on him; and to our God, for He will abundantly pardon' (Isa. 55:6, 7). Similarly, the Apostle Paul proclaimed, 'Behold, now is the accepted time; behold, now is the day of salvation' (2 Cor. 6:2).

Salvation is the most important and urgent matter of all. Pop singer Michael Jackson – now deceased – was once criticized for dangling his baby over a high balcony. Putting off believing in Jesus, however, is dangling with your immortal soul. Time is brief. Eternity is near. Scripture states 'It is appointed for men to die once, but after this the judgment' (Heb. 9:27). The summons of the gospel is 'Believe on the Lord Jesus Christ, and you will be saved' (Acts 16:31). Decisions in time have eternal consequences. The difference between spending eternity in heaven or spending it in hell is determined by coming to saving faith in the Lord Jesus Christ in time. After our last breath there is no further opportunity to trust Christ for salvation.

> *Life at best is very brief,*
> *Like the falling of a leaf,*
> *Like the binding of a sheaf,*
> *Be in time.*
>
> *Fleeting days are telling fast,*
> *That the die will soon be cast,*
> *And the fatal line be passed,*
> *Be in time.*

Make hay while the sun shines

Be in time, be in time,
While the voice of Jesus calls you, be in time.
If in sin you longer wait,
You may find no open gate,
And your cry be just too late, be in time.

(ANON.)

The Christian

The Bible also urges Christians to 'make hay while the sun shines'. The application here is to make the most of every opportunity the Lord gives us, being good stewards of the time, energy and opportunity the Lord bestows on us – in C. T. Studd's memorable words, 'Only one life, 'twill soon be past, only what's done for Christ will last.'

While we are saved by faith, faith works! We are saved to serve. Paul exhorts all believers, 'See then that you walk circumspectly, not as fools but as wise, redeeming the time, because the days are evil' (Eph. 5:15, 16). God has a plan for every Christian's life, and God has a work for every Christian to do. He only requires that we are faithful to our individual calling, within the limits of the circumstances He has ordained for us and the abilities He has given to us. 'We are His workmanship, created in Christ Jesus for good works, which God prepared beforehand that we should walk in them' (Eph. 2:10).

No Christian, then, is exempt from divine service. You are the only you. 'Make hay while the sun shines.' Beware of the trivial. Beware of distractions. Keep the Lord always before you:

There's a work for Jesus,
Ready at your hand;
'Tis a task the Master
Just for you has planned.

A Little Bird Told Me

Haste to do His bidding,
Yield Him service true;
There's a work for Jesus
None but you can do.

(ELSIE DUNCAN YALE, 1873–1956)

The late Bishop J. C. Ryle once wrote the following rallying call to all Christians:

> *The Lord Jesus bids you 'occupy'. By that He means that you are to be a 'doer' in your Christianity, and not merely a hearer and professor. He wants His servants not only to receive His wages, and eat His bread, and dwell in His home, and belong to His family – but also to do His work. You are to 'let your light so shine before men that they may see your good works.' Have you faith? It must not be a dead faith; it must 'work by love'. Are you elect? You are elect unto 'obedience'. Are you redeemed? You are redeemed that you may be 'a peculiar people, zealous of good works'. Do you love Christ? Prove the reality of your love by keeping Christ's commandments. Oh, reader, do not forget this charge to 'occupy'.[1]*

'Make hay while the sun shines.' The statement is not in the Bible, but, paradoxically, the statement is eminently biblical in its spirit of urgency. It is a warning to non-Christians to believe and be saved while they may. And it is an exhortation to Christians to invest for eternity and 'redeem the time' for the glory of God.

---

1. J.C. Ryle, *Occupy Until I Come!*, from *Coming Events and Present Duties – Being Plain Papers on Prophecy*, 1879, from http://gracegems.org/Ryle/coming_events_and_present_duties3.htm, accessed 22 March 2014

52

The half has not been told!

'You haven't heard the half of it!' We sometimes use this expression when we relate our experience to someone who has only heard about our experience second-hand. They have the gist of it, but not the full story. The experience could be a wonderful one or a terrible one. We send a postcard to a friend from an exotic holiday location. 'Having a wonderful time …' When we return home, they ask us more about our holiday. 'It was far more exciting than we could portray on the back of a postcard,' we tell them. 'The half has not been told.' Conversely, we meet a war veteran. We have read the historical accounts of war, but he knows what it was like at ground level. A companion of his was killed by a roadside booby-trap bomb. He finds it difficult to talk about the reality of war. 'Hopefully, you will never know the reality,' he says to us. 'The half has not been told.'

The Queen of Sheba

The expression 'The half has not been told' originates from the lips of the Queen of Sheba in the tenth century B.C., as related in the Old Testament. Sheba is located in south-west Arabia, modern-day Yemen. The Queen of Sheba had heard about the wisdom and reputation of King Solomon in Israel, and was so intrigued that she travelled over a thousand miles to meet him in Jerusalem. She wished to satisfy her curiosity and possibly, also, to make a trade agreement. Israel at that time was enjoying an unrivalled economic prosperity – although, sadly, under King Solomon, a spiritual decline was starting to set in.

The Queen of Sheba's visit to Israel surpassed her wildest expectations and imagination. Upon quizzing King Solomon, she found that he actually was as wise as the reports had suggested. She thus exclaimed: 'It was a true report which I heard in my own land about your words and your wisdom. However I did not believe the words until I came and saw with my own eyes; and indeed *the half was not told me.* Your wisdom and prosperity exceed the fame of which I heard' (1 Kings 10:6, 7, emphasis mine).

A Spiritual Application

'The half was not told me.' We can apply this expression in a spiritual sense. When we come to saving faith in Christ, and know the joy of salvation, it is a case of 'the half has not been told'. We just did not realize that before we trusted Christ, we were only half alive – we were alive physically, but dead spiritually. We were dead to God. But the Bible says, 'Therefore, if anyone is in Christ, he is a new creation; old things have passed away; behold, all things have become new' (2 Cor. 5:17).

The Christian faith is an evangelistic faith. Good news is for sharing. Remember there is a hell to be shunned, a heaven to be gained and a Saviour who saves. Yet describing the joy of salvation to a non-Christian is akin to describing a beautiful sunset to a blind person or a Beethoven symphony to one who is deaf. It is greater than words can tell. It has been said truly that

> *Heaven above is softer blue,*
> *Earth around is sweeter green;*
> *Something lives in every hue*
> *Christless eyes have never seen:*
> *Birds with gladder songs o'erflow,*
> *Flow'rs with deeper beauties shine,*
> *Since I know, as now I know,*
> *I am His, and He is mine.*

(GEORGE WADE ROBINSON, 1838–77)

A Celestial Application

When the Christian reaches glory, and sees the Saviour face to face, surely then it will also be a case of 'The half has not been told.' We will realize afresh the cost of our redemption. We will realize anew the depths of the Saviour's love, and the splendour of heaven will exceed our greatest expectation. We will be forced to exclaim, 'The half has not been told.' 'Eye has not seen, nor ear heard, nor have entered into the heart of man the things which God has prepared for those who love Him' (1 Cor. 2:9).

What will heaven be like? It will be greater and more glorious than tongue can presently tell. But for the Christian, heaven is home – the place of safety, peace, rest and contentment. Jesus said, 'In My Father's house are many rooms [lit. 'abiding places']. If it were not so, would I have told you that I go to prepare a place for you?' (John 14:2 ESV). In the Father's house – that is, in God's nearer presence – we shall be eternally saved, eternally safe and eternally satisfied. '[Nothing] … will be able to separate us from the love of God in Christ Jesus our Lord' (Rom. 8:39, ESV). Our fellowship with God our Maker will be without hindrance and without handicap. Our joy will have no end. We will be able finally to fulfil our chief end of glorifying God and enjoying Him for ever. When it comes to the Christian's future blessedness, truly, 'The half has not been told!'

SOLI DEO GLORIA

Christian Focus Publications

Our mission statement –

STAYING FAITHFUL
In dependence upon God we seek to impact the world through literature faithful to His infallible Word, the Bible. Our aim is to ensure that the Lord Jesus Christ is presented as the only hope to obtain forgiveness of sin, live a useful life and look forward to heaven with Him.

Our books are published in four imprints:

CHRISTIAN
FOCUS

Popular works including biographies, commentaries, basic doctrine and Christian living.

CHRISTIAN
HERITAGE

Books representing some of the best material from the rich heritage of the church.

MENTOR

Books written at a level suitable for Bible College and seminary students, pastors, and other serious readers. The imprint includes commentaries, doctrinal studies, examination of current issues and church history.

CF4•K

Children's books for quality Bible teaching and for all age groups: Sunday school curriculum, puzzle and activity books; personal and family devotional titles, biographies and inspirational stories – because you are never too young to know Jesus!

Christian Focus Publications Ltd,
Geanies House, Fearn, Ross-shire,
IV20 1TW, Scotland, United Kingdom.
www.christianfocus.com
blog.christianfocus.com